AF807334

FEDERAL RESERVE BEHAVIOR, 1923–1931

MARSHALL E. MCMAHON

Routledge
Taylor & Francis Group
LONDON AND NEW YORK

First published in 1993 by Garland Publishing, Inc.

This edition first published in 2018
by Routledge
2 Park Square, Milton Park, Abingdon, Oxon OX14 4RN

and by Routledge
711 Third Avenue, New York, NY 10017

Routledge is an imprint of the Taylor & Francis Group, an informa business

© 1993 Marshall E. McMahon

All rights reserved. No part of this book may be reprinted or reproduced or utilised in any form or by any electronic, mechanical, or other means, now known or hereafter invented, including photocopying and recording, or in any information storage or retrieval system, without permission in writing from the publishers.

Trademark notice: Product or corporate names may be trademarks or registered trademarks, and are used only for identification and explanation without intent to infringe.

British Library Cataloguing in Publication Data
A catalogue record for this book is available from the British Library

ISBN: 978-1-138-70169-4 (Set)
ISBN: 978-1-315-10595-6 (Set) (ebk)
ISBN: 978-1-138-08724-8 (Volume 7) (hbk)
ISBN: 978-1-315-10935-0 (Volume 7) (ebk)

Publisher's Note
The publisher has gone to great lengths to ensure the quality of this reprint but points out that some imperfections in the original copies may be apparent.

Disclaimer
The publisher has made every effort to trace copyright holders and would welcome correspondence from those they have been unable to trace.

FEDERAL RESERVE BEHAVIOR 1923–1931

MARSHALL E. McMAHON

GARLAND PUBLISHING, INC.
NEW YORK & LONDON
1993

Copyright © 1993 by Marshall E. McMahon
All rights reserved

Library of Congress Cataloging-in-Publication Data

McMahon, Marshall E., 1944–
Federal Reserve behavior, 1923–1931 / by Marshall E. McMahon.
p. cm. — (Financial sector of the American economy)
Revision of thesis (Ph.D.)—Vanderbilt University, 1972.
Includes bibliographical references (p.) and index.
ISBN 0–8153–0965–1 (alk. paper)
1. Board of Governors of the Federal Reserve System (U.S.)—History. 2. Monetary policy—United States—History.
I. Title. II. Series.
HG2563.M33 1993
332.1'1'0973—dc20 92-35292
CIP

Printed on acid-free, 250-year-life paper
Manufactured in the United States of America

To Betty

Who believes in me
even when I don't
believe in myself

Tables

Preface

It had been almost 20 years since Vanderbilt University had accepted my doctoral thesis when Mr. Jonathan Oestreich invited me to submit the work for inclusion in Garland's dissertation series on the Financial Sector. I was as pleased as I was surprised. In the two decades since I had completed my doctoral work, my academic career had unfolded much more in the direction of teaching and administration than in the area of research—as much by plan as by fortune. Indeed, it had been nearly as long since I had even *read* my dissertation! (I was tempted to designate these preliminary comments a "Foreword" instead of a "Preface" because I certainly feel like a different person than the young man who wrote the dissertation that follows.)

When I accepted a position at Rhodes College (at that time, Southwestern At Memphis) in 1972, the same year I received my Ph.D., there was so little emphasis placed on publication that I put all my effort into teaching and largely abandoned my research interest in Federal Reserve policy in the 1920's and 1930's. Precisely for that reason, I was really quite unfamiliar with the work that had been done on the topic since 1972. Fortunately, a recent work by David C. Wheelock, based on his 1987 doctoral dissertation at the University of Illinois, remedied this deficiency (*The Srategy and Consistency of Federal Reseve Monetary Policy, 1924-1933*, Cambridge: Cambridge University Press, 1991). Not only does Wheelock review the studies published in the years after the acceptance of my dissertation, he also adds the fruits of his own commendable efforts to what we know about the failure of the Fed to "do something" about the Great Depression before it reached the depths that it did. The reader who—after reading the present work, of course—wishes to know more about the work done since 1972 would do well to look into Wheelock's book.

In the pre-1970 literature on Federal Reserve behavior during the period in question, investigators had relied almost exclusively on the accounts of participants and observers during the 1920's and 1930's. Where data were used to attempt to sort through the various accounts, they were used in a very casual way. It was my intention to use more rigorous quantitative techniques in my dissertation to attempt to sort out some of the conflicting contemporary testimony.

Briefly, I concluded that the Fed did not handle the downturn of 1929 as well as it might have primarily because Fed officials were relying on financial indicators and experience that proved to be of little value in such completely new circumstances and because they were afraid of rekindling speculation on the stock market. While open market operations and the Fed's rate policies (changes in the discount and acceptance rates at the New York Fed) did turn mildly expansionary in November and December, 1929, in response to both the decline in output and the stock market crash, the Fed did not continue to make substantial open market purchases into 1930 and 1931. Reductions in the discount and acceptance buying rates continued until October, 1931, when both rates were *raised* substantially. In late September, 1931, Britain had abandoned the gold standard and the United States began to lose a substantial amount of its monetary gold stock. In response, the Fed raised both the discount and acceptance rates in an effort to stem the loss of gold. Of course, one has to wonder if, even in the early 1930's, the discount and acceptance rates were sufficiently powerful tools that the reductions could have had much impact on the disastrous course of events. At the same time, however, it seems to be quite clear that the Fed's exclusive attention to international considerations in late 1931, to the detriment of domestic concerns, was a serious policy error.

In the 1920's, Fed officials had developed the habit of looking at market interest rates to determine the state of the market for credit. After October, 1929, short-term rates fell substantially until the shift in Fed policy in October, 1931. For example, the open market rate on 4-6 month commercial paper in New York fell from 6.25% in October, 1929, to 3.00% in August, 1930; and by October, 1931, it had fallen to 2.00%. Given what Fed officials thought they had learned from earlier experience, there seemed to be little reason for the Fed to pursue a policy of aggressive purchases and more rapid reductions in the discount and acceptance rates. Furthermore, the decline in industrial production appeared to have stopped early in 1930, and, as previously indicated, Fed officials worried that too much easing of credit would simply fuel renewed speculation on the stock market, which was showing at least some signs of stabilizing early in 1930.

In terms of some of the other issues in the literature prior to 1972, my research supported the conclusions that (1.) *both* domestic and international considerations (essentially, the restoration and preservation of the gold standard) were important in the setting of Fed policy throughout the period in question, and (2.) there was no radical change in Federal Reserve behavior associated with the waning of the influence of Benjamin Strong, Governor of the Reserve Bank of New York and de facto leader of the Fed during most of the 1920's. It also appeared to me that, throughout the entire period 1923-1931, the Fed relied more on changes in the discount and acceptance rates (especially the latter) in pursuit of its international objectives and used open market operations for its domestic countercyclical efforts. Furthermore, there is some evidence that the Fed may have used the discount rate (but not the acceptance rate) in combination with open market operations to combat stock market speculation. Finally, as a side issue, my research indicated that defensive open market operations, designed to "protect" member bank reserves from undesired changes attributable to external sources, were non-existent during the period examined. Instead, there is some evidence that defensive operations were conducted by member banks themselves through changes in the amount of bankers' acceptances presented to the Fed for discounting.

In my research, I used two different models of Federal Reserve behavior to test several hypotheses gleaned from previous works and the minutes of the Open Market Investment Committee. The derivation of the reduced-form equations (one for each policy variable in each model) proceeded from the formulation of two different, but similar, quadratic disutility functions in which the disutility of Fed policymakers was assumed to depend on the differences between the desired and actual values of the variables Fed officials wished to affect. In the first model, the disutilty function included only the desired and actual levels of a short-term interest rate. In the second model, disutility was related to the desired and actual values of four ultimate target variables: output, international gold flows, speculation in commodities, and speculation on the stock market. In each model, allowance was also made for the possibility that Fed officials might have preferred *not* to act. The reduced-form equations for each policy variable were then derived by minimizing the respective disutility functions subject to the constraints imposed by the way Fed officials thought their actions affected the variables they wished to influence.

David Wheelock, working independently fifteen years later, undertook his study for many of the same reasons I had chosen to work on the topic. He, too, was dissatisfied with the lack of rigorous quantitative testing of hypotheses in many of the same works I had used. However, rather than proceeding through the mental gymnastics described in the preceding paragraph, Wheelock went straight to the formulation of reaction functions for each of the policy variables. While the specific formulations of the equations for each policy variable and the exact definitions of the variables used were different in each of the studies, there are, as one would expect, substantial similarities in both approaches.

There are also significant similarities in the conclusions concerning issues that we both addressed. Wheelock finds evidence of the importance of both domestic considerations (output and speculation) and international considerations (gold flow) in the formulation of Fed policy, and he fails to find support for the belief in a dramatic change in Fed policy associated (in time, anyway) with Strong's waning influence. Wheelock also concludes that the Fed's failure to respond adequately to the onset of the Great Depression was largely the result of its failure to interpret indicators of credit market conditions correctly. In these important respects, our results are very much the same.

However, there are also some differences in our conclusions. Wheelock found substantial similarity in the Fed's reaction, by way of each of its policy variables, to changes in the domestic and international variables it wanted to influence, whereas I found what appear to be significant differences in the Fed's use of open market operations, changes in the discount rate, and changes in the acceptance rate in its attempts to influence domestic and international economic and financial conditions. Additionally, Wheelock attributes the Fed's failure to interpret credit market conditions correctly to its focus on member bank borrowings instead of interest rates and concludes from a detailed analysis of member bank borrowing that this focus gave Fed policy a decidedly procyclical slant. Finally, Wheelock addresses a number of other important questions in his study that I did not address in mine. Of particular note is Wheelock's examination of some of the organizational changes and ambiguities in, as well as conflicts within, the System, during this period.

In the dissertation that follows, I have made no changes of substance and only minor changes in style—primarily only in the most awkward and obscure phrasing that I found on reentering its domain. However, even this minimally revised version would not have been possible were it not for the tireless effort, patience, and good humor of Marci Hendrix. I also want to thank Trey Clark for his magical reincarnation of the charts in Appendix B, Jonathan Oestreich for asking me to submit the dissertation for consideration, and Stuart Bruchey for finding it worthy of publication.

Acknowledgments

This dissertation was written under the supervision of Professor Ben Bolch. I want to thank him not only for his constant advice and suggestions but also for his encouragement and gentle prodding. I also want to thank Professor Rendigs Fels for his criticisms of the original draft and for his interest and guidance throughout my graduate career.

Federal Reserve Behavior 1923–1931

CHAPTER ONE

Introduction

The Federal Reserve System (Fed) has been widely criticized for its response (or lack of response) to the economic and financial problems of the period 1928-1933. This period, as is well known, was one of frantic speculation, followed by the collapse of the stock market, the banking system, and the economy at large, and ending in the declaration of a national banking holiday by President Franklin Roosevelt. It is not difficult to understand why Federal Reserve behavior has been the subject of many scholarly investigations. Some scholars ask how the System could have allowed these events to happen; others put it more strongly and ask what perverse behavior led the System to "cause" such a widespread collapse.

The failure of the System and its officials has frequently been viewed as the result of incompetent leadership, usually with the implication that had Benjamin Strong (Governor of the New York Federal Reserve Bank until his death in October, 1928) lived, the Fed would have performed much better. This conclusion is based largely on the Fed's successful actions in the period 1923-1928, during which time monetary policy was apparently used to combat two minor recessions. This hypothesis is carefully formulated by Milton Friedman and Anna Schwartz in their monumental *Monetary History of the United States, 1867-1960.*[1]

In opposition to the belief that Federal Reserve behavior was "inconsistent" before and after 1928, two alternative theories have recently been offered. It is the contention of Elmus R. Wicker that Federal Reserve behavior was consistent throughout the period, and that the primary objective of the Fed was international financial stabilization.[2] Karl Brunner and Allan Meltzer contend that Federal Reserve behavior was consistent, but that the goals of Federal Reserve policy were domestic in character. They believe that the failure of the Fed in the years 1928-1933 was the result of the incorrect conception of the workings of monetary policy, which accidentally led Fed officials to correct decisions and actions in the earlier years (1923-1927), but failed to do so in the later years (1928-1933). Brunner and Meltzer believe that the behavior was consistent while the effects of the behavior varied.[3]

The conclusions that have been drawn in these studies have been based largely on the public and private statements of Fed officials. This is, of course, a valid approach to the problem. There are, however, many subjective problems of interpretation in any such undertaking. The diversity of opinion among the conclusions referred to above is ample evidence of the problems involved. While the authors used many of the same sources, they came to very different conclusions.[4]

Given that this approach has led to widely diverse conclusions, it is of great import which, if any, of these conclusions is supported by a statistical analysis of the relevant data. As John H. Wood has maintained:

> Analyses of statements and publications issuing from the Federal Reserve cannot provide "proof" that the monetary authorities act in any specified manner. . . . But these statements and publications can be useful insofar as they are "suggestive" of hypotheses which might then be tested in more systematic ways, that is, by analyses of the behavior, as opposed to the statements, of policy makers.[5]

This is precisely the purpose of this thesis.

The approach followed in the present investigation is the formulation of hypotheses regarding Federal Reserve behavior in the period 1923-1931, based on original and secondary sources, followed by statistical testing of the hypotheses. As will become evident, there are many problems in this approach; but it is only through such an attempt that the controversy can possibly be resolved.

Chapter Two provides a summary of the arguments briefly referred to above and adds to these arguments additional evidence from other sources. It is, in other words, a verbal statement of the divergent views and a synthesis of these views which incorporates the work of other authors and of the Fed officials involved. The chapter ends with a verbal statement of the hypotheses to be tested.

In Chapter Three the hypotheses are quantified and tested, in various forms, using regression analysis. This approach provides direct evidence on the Wicker and Brunner-Meltzer hypotheses, but only indirect evidence can be obtained on the Friedman-Schwartz hypothesis. Nevertheless, conclusions can be drawn regarding each of these hypotheses from the results presented in Chapter Three. Chapter Four is a summary chapter which presents the conclusions obtained from the study.

Two of the three appendices do not provide any additional evidence on the primary questions that the study attempts to answer: Appendix A contains a list of the data used in the statistical tests and the sources of this data; Appendix C contains the mathematical derivations for the models presented in Chapter Three. Appendix B does, however, contain some evidence on the behavior of Fed officials and member banks in the period 1923-1931. This appendix contains a spectral analysis of the important components of the Reserve equation which leads to some interesting observations regarding the fluctuations in these components.

NOTES

1. Milton Friedman and Anna J. Schwartz. 1958. *A Monetary History of the United States, 1867-1960* (Princeton: Princeton University Press, pp. 407-19). Lester Chandler may also be counted among those supporting this view, although less strongly than Friedman and Schwartz. See Lester V. Chandler. 1958. *Benjamin Strong, Central Banker* (Washington, D.C.: The Brookings Institution).

2. Elmus R. Wicker. "Federal Reserve Monetary Policy, 1922-1933: A Reinterpretation." *Journal of Political Economy*, LXXIII (August 1965), pp. 324-43. See also his *Federal Reserve Monetary Policy, 1917-1933* (New York: Random House, 1966).

3. Karl Brunner and Allan H. Meltzer, "What Did We Learn From the Monetary Experience of the United States in the Great Depression?" *Canadian Journal of Economics*, I (May, 1968), pp. 334-48.

_____, *The Federal Reserve's Attachment to the Free Reserve Concept: A Staff Analysis* (Report of the Subcommittee on Domestic Finance, Committee on Banking and Currency, House of Representatives, 88th Congress; 2nd Session) (Washington, D.C.: U.S. Government Printing Office, 1964).

4. It may also be persuasively argued that the statements of Fed officials at any moment in time may be misleading as to the long run behavioral pattern of the decision makers. As Charles O. Hardy observed, it is common for officials to fortify their decisions with a myriad of reasons for coming to a given policy whether or not all the factors cited entered the original decision-making process. (Charles O. Hardy, *Credit Policies of the Federal Reserve System* (Washington, D.C.: The Brookings Institution, 1932, p. 108).

5. John H. Wood, "A Model of Federal Reserve Behavior," in George Horwich, ed., *Monetary Process and Policy: A Symposium* (Homewood: Richard D. Irwin, Inc., 1967, p. 144). Wood also states that, in his view, the statements and publications of the Fed and its officials cannot ". . . even constitute useful evidence to be applied

toward hypotheses of Federal Reserve behavior." (Ibid.) I do not agree with this contention. As is made clear in the conclusions of this study, it is my belief that neither type of evidence (analysis of statements versus statistical analysis of behavior) can or should stand alone. Rather, both kinds of evidence should be used and evaluated before any conclusions are reached.

CHAPTER TWO

Federal Reserve Behavior: A Verbal Analysis

The purpose of this chapter is to describe briefly the alternative theories of Federal Reserve behavior referred to in the introduction. The major differences between the theories are emphasized, additional information is included, and finally a synthesis is attempted in hopes of arriving at testable hypotheses about Federal Reserve behavior.

Friedman and Schwartz's Theory of Inconsistent Behavior

Prior to his death in October, 1928, Benjamin Strong had been the dominant figure in the Federal Reserve System. As Governor of the Federal Reserve Bank of New York, Strong held a key position of authority in the System. New York City was the national and international financial center of the 1920's, and Strong's influence helped to shape both national and international monetary policy. His biographer, Lester Chandler, has described him as:

> . . . one of the world's most influential leaders in the fields of money and finance. During the first fourteen turbulent, formative years of the Federal Reserve System, his was the greatest influence on American monetary and banking policies; he had no close competitor.[1]

In short, the Fed had a leader in its early years who had a vast experience with the problems of national and international finance and who shaped its policies prior to 1929 more than any other individual.

It is not difficult to believe, therefore, that the loss of such a man would be a disruptive factor in the formulation and execution of Federal Reserve policy. But Friedman and Schwartz have gone much farther than this. They contend that there was a *definite contrast* between Federal Reserve policy before and after 1929, and that the reason for this contrast was the death of Benjamin Strong and the subsequent " . . . shift of power within the System and the lack of understanding and experience of the individuals to whom the power shifted."[2] After Strong's death, a struggle for power ensued in which the Federal Reserve Board gained control over the System. Strong's successor as Governor of the New York Fed, George Harrison, at first fought for control of the System and for an expansionary policy; but he lacked the persuasion and the experience to succeed Strong as the leader of the System.[3]

Even if Harrison had succeeded in keeping the New York Fed the de facto center of the System, Friedman and Schwartz doubt that he could have been much more successful than the Board in preventing the collapse of the banking system. They conclude from their analysis that only Strong could have provided the knowledge to deal with the crises that developed after 1929 and the force to transform this knowledge into policy. After his death, there was no one with the experience and power to carry through the kind of program that was necessary to stave off the collapse of the banking system.[4] And it was the failure of the banks that provided " . . . the mechanism through which a drastic decline was produced in the stock of money."[5]

The theory of Friedman and Schwartz is therefore that Federal Reserve policy changed after 1929 because the leadership of the Fed changed. In particular, after Strong's death, the leadership of the Fed passed to people who were far less capable of pursuing policies appropriate to economic and financial recovery because of a lack of understanding of the economic system.

Wicker's "International" Theory

In contrast to the theory of Friedman and Schwartz, Wicker's main thesis is that, for Strong and his successors, " . . . domestic considerations were significant for the determination of monetary policy only when they happened to coincide or did not conflict with international considerations, namely, the maintenance of gold convertibility of European currencies."[6] In other words, international goals received the largest weight in the development of Federal Reserve policy. Domestic considerations were given a much lower priority.

It is Wicker's contention that the *timing* of the purchases and sales of government securities was a function of the differential between the short term interest rates in New York and London and that the *volume* of purchases and sales was a function of gold imports. Since gold imports were a positive function of the New York-London interest rate differential, open market operations were undertaken to reduce this differential in order to reduce gold imports and hence to enable England first to return to, and then remain on, the gold standard. At the same time, gold imports that did occur were viewed as increasing the possibility of inflation *in the future* and were therefore met with open market purchases to increase the stock of securities that could later be sold to combat inflation. Such purchases also helped to drive down interest rates and stem the gold inflows resulting from capital investment by the British in the New York markets.[7]

The "anti-recession" open market operations of the Fed in 1924 and 1927 were, according to Wicker, actually designed and executed to establish " . . . an appropriate interest rate differential between New York and London for the purpose of reversing the gold flow . . . ."[8] The failure of the Fed to purchase large amounts of securities in 1930 was *not* an inconsistent reaction to recession but a result of the same policy that prevailed in 1924 and 1927. But in 1930, " . . . the international gold standard was not in imminent danger, and concern about controlling future inflation was not serious."[9]

The method by which open market operations influenced interest rates was spelled out in what Wicker calls the Burgess-Strong doctrine. According to this theory, the extension of credit by member banks was limited by the debt of the member banks. Member banks, because of the System tradition against borrowing, did not like to borrow from the Fed and did so only out of necessity. When member banks were in debt to the Fed, then credit conditions were tight and interest rates tended to rise. The opposite was true when member banks did not have large borrowings from the Fed.

Federal Reserve purchases of government securities enabled the banks to pay off their debts to the Fed. Being less in debt, the banks as a whole were more willing to lend, and interest rates fell (ceteris paribus).

Based on this theory of how open market operations work and the great importance of the New York and Chicago money centers, Wicker concludes that "[t]he objective of open market purchases . . . was limited to . . . eliminating the indebtedness of the member banks in New York and Chicago."[10]

Wicker does not ignore domestic considerations, nor does he believe them to have been of no importance to the policy makers.[11] He states that the policy makers were interested in obtaining "maximum output" (capacity output?) and in stemming price inflation that was not accompanied by increases in output.

To obtain these domestic goals, the policy makers' desired volume of credit was governed by the volume of output. Price increases were not avoided per se; price increases accompanied by increasing output were not objectionable.[12]

Nevertheless, the thrust of Wicker's argument is clear: the goals of the Fed during the entire period were international in character; domestic goals were practically inconsequential.

The "Domestic" Theory of Brunner and Meltzer

According to Brunner and Meltzer, the goals of the Fed were domestic throughout the period 1922-1933. Federal Reserve behavior was consistent, but the consequences of that behavior varied. Because of an incorrect conception of how monetary policy worked, the Fed failed to respond adequately to the depression that started in 1929.[13]

The manner in which Federal Reserve policy makers thought their actions (open market operations) affected interest rates and, therefore, commercial bank loans, is expressed in the authors' interpretation of the

Riefler-Burgess doctrine. Open market purchases were accompanied by decreased member-bank borrowing since such purchases provided the means for member banks to pay off their costly debts and still maintain the necessary reserves. Their "improved" position then led the commercial banks to lend at lower rates, and the public was thereby induced to borrow. Open market sales worked in a symmetrical way to increase borrowing, which led to increased interest rates (as the member banks' reserves were composed more and more of borrowing from the Fed) and therefore to less credit provided to the public.[14]

Short term interest rates were taken as the indicator of credit conditions. The necessity to undertake open market operations was indicated by the level of short-term interest rates and the direction of recent changes in these rates. Likewise, changes in short-term rates indicated the success of such operations. The volume of open market purchases or sales necessary was indicated by the current volume of member bank borrowing since borrowing determined interest rates.[15]

Brunner and Meltzer provide evidence for their theory by looking at data on short-term interest rates, purchases and sales of government securities and acceptances, and borrowing from the Fed for a twenty-month period following each of the peaks in 1923, 1926, and 1929. In none of the declines were purchases sufficient to offset decreased borrowings, but more purchases were not undertaken because of the apparent "ease" in the money market as reflected in declining short-term interest rates.

Federal Reserve policy failed more severely after 1929 than after the other two peaks because the extended monetary base fell during the 1929 debacle whereas it had not changed or had risen in the two previous recessions. Since the extended base is the main determinant of the stock of money, monetary policy in 1929-30 was in fact restrictive.[16]

While Brunner and Meltzer never spell out exactly what the goals of monetary policy were during this period, it is probably safe to assume that these goals were the expansion of output and the control of inflation. In other words, Federal Reserve policy was meant to be counter cyclical. The authors feel that international considerations did not play a role in the formulation of the policies of the 1920's and early 1930's.[17]

Similarities and Differences in the Alternative Explanations

All of the authors whose theories have been summarized above seem to agree on how the Fed thought open market operations affected the money market. They differ primarily in the goals they believe the Fed was pursuing and/or in the belief that the Fed's actions in the pursuit of those goals were consistent before and after 1929. There are other differences that also need to be made clear.

The basic similarity is in the belief that the Fed was following the Riefler-Burgess (or Burgess-Strong) explanation of the effect of open market operations.[18] This explanation rests on the belief that member banks were reluctant to borrow from the Reserve Banks because of the System tradition against borrowing for more than very short periods of time. Member banks were encouraged to borrow for "legitimate" needs, but continuous debt at the Reserve Bank was frowned upon. Consequently, the doctrine states, member banks were reluctant to lend or to invest when they were in debt but were quite willing to do so when they were virtually out of debt. This led to a positive relationship between short-term interest rates and the debt of member banks, ceteris paribus.

The effect of open market purchases was to reduce the debt of member banks by providing the means to pay off the debt. The result was a greater willingness to lend and lower interest rates. Conversely, the effect of open market sales was to increase the debt of member banks by forcing them to borrow to maintain their reserves. The result in this case was a greater hesitancy in lending (and perhaps a reduction in lending) and higher interest rates. (All this assumes, of course, that other things, including other sources and uses of reserve funds and the demand for credit, remain the same.)[19]

The primary differences center, of course, on the questions of goals and consistency of behavior. Brunner and Meltzer and Friedman and Schwartz reject the theory that international considerations were important at any time other than when they happened to call for the same policy as did domestic considerations.[20] Wicker believes just the opposite: the only time domestic conditions were considered was when they happened to require the same policy as did international conditions.[21]

However, on the question of consistent policy, Brunner and Meltzer and Wicker believe that policy was consistent throughout the period. Friedman and Schwartz contend that there was a discontinuity in the policy due to the death of Benjamin Strong.[22] On this question, then, the authors side differently than on the question of goals.

There are, in addition to the differences highlighted above, other contradictions in the various accounts of Federal Reserve behavior. When Wicker refers to open market purchases and sales, he apparently means purchases and sales of government securities only (although this is not always clear).[23] But Brunner and Meltzer cite data on purchases and sales of both government securities and bills bought (acceptances) as the open market policy variable.[24] In the criticism in the next section, this point is explored further.

Finally, there is one other difference between Wicker and Brunner and Meltzer on the one hand, and Friedman and Schwartz on the other. It is entirely possible that the two camps are talking about slightly different things when they disagree over the importance of the death of Benjamin Strong.

Friedman and Schwartz clearly state that there was a ". . . contrast between Federal Reserve policy before 1929 and after. . ."[25] and it is on this point that Wicker[26] and Brunner and Meltzer[27] focus their attack. The real question raised by Wicker and Brunner and Meltzer is why the Fed did not react with more vigorous open market purchases after the downturn in business in late 1929. This is the question on which this thesis provides additional evidence.

But the question that Friedman and Schwartz ask goes somewhat beyond that. They admit that:

> The men who established the Federal Reserve System had many misconceptions about monetary theory and banking operations. It may well be that a policy in accordance with their understanding of monetary matters would not have prevented the decline in the stock of money from 1929 to the end of 1930.[28]

But their main point is that these founders (including, of course, Benjamin Strong) would *not* have allowed the banking panics to develop and "... would have cut short the liquidity crisis before it had gone very far, perhaps before the end of 1930."[29]

It is not clear that Friedman and Schwartz believe Strong would have acted soon enough to stop the contraction. What they do emphasize is that, based especially on his experiences in 1907, he would never have let the banking crisis become so severe.[30] To the extent that the two can be separated (the general contraction and the financial collapse), it appears that Friedman and Schwartz believe Strong would have provided the necessary leadership to prevent the financial collapse; but it is not clear that they believe that his actions concerning the general contraction in late 1929 and in 1930 would necessarily have been greatly different from those of his successors.

The term "inconsistent" is therefore not completely accurate in describing the Friedman-Schwartz hypothesis. The hypothesis includes more than the apparent incongruity of Federal Reserve behavior before and after 1929; it involves also the question of a response to a totally different situation. Obviously, a response to a unique event (in this case, the bank failures) cannot be classified as "consistent" or "inconsistent."[31]

Brunner and Meltzer do not explicitly consider the problem of the bank failures, and their analysis of Federal Reserve open market operations ends in early 1931.[32] While Wicker refers to the later period (1931-1933) in part of his article, he too largely ignores the bank failures and emphasizes the policy of the Fed prior to the most serious banking crisis.[33]

The point is simply this: It is conceivably true that Federal Reserve policy was consistent in the entire period from 1923 to early 1931 and yet that Benjamin Strong, had he lived, would have been able to provide the necessary influence to sufficiently change Federal Reserve policy after early 1931 to prevent the widespread collapse of the banking system in 1933.

Of course, it is *not* possible to separate the banking crises and the contraction completely--they were intimately related. But the lack of official concern over the banking failures indicates that Fed officials managed to keep the two isolated to some extent in their decisions.[34] Perhaps this is where Benjamin Strong would have provided the most valuable aid.

Criticism

It is not easy to find fault with Friedman and Schwartz. These authors build a strong case for what is essentially an untestable hypothesis with respect to the bank failures. The greatest criticism of their explanation for the change in Federal Reserve behavior they themselves anticipate.[35] That criticism is, of course, that it is difficult to believe that one man could have saved the country from the collapse it experienced in the 1930's. On the other hand, it does appear to be true that Strong dominated the System prior to his death; and it is also true that he gained experience in the banking panic of 1907 that would undoubtedly have been valuable in the early 1930's.[36] But Friedman and Schwartz also admit that many leading economists who had also gone through the earlier crisis were practically oblivious to the existence of the later crisis.[37]

It can never be proved that Strong would have been able to prevent the collapse of the banking system or that he would have failed to do so. This question simply cannot be answered. It is, however, possible to examine *indirectly* the question of inconsistent response to the depression itself.

It is argued by Friedman and Schwartz[38] and by Chandler[39] that Strong would have eased the restrictive credit policy of 1928-29 before the stock market crash. This restrictictive policy was unquestionably initiated to try to stop the speculation on the stock market and Strong initially concurred in this effort.[40] But based on earlier statements and statements made shortly before his death, these authors conclude that Strong would not have pushed such a restrictive policy for as long as his successors did. Chandler cites a letter written by Strong in August of 1928 indicating that he might have led the New York Fed to an easier money policy even if the System as a whole disagreed.[41]

Unfortunately Benjamin Strong did not live long enough to provide the leadership that Friedman and Schwartz and Chandler believe he would have provided. In fact, it is doubtful that Strong had much influence on the System after early 1928. He was in Europe from May to August of that year and died shortly after his return.[42]

While it is difficult to test the hypothesis of inconsistent behavior explicitly, an attempt is made to shed some light on the question in

Chapter Three. At present, all that can be said is that the hypothesis is appealing, but strains the imagination to some extent.[43]

Wicker's explanation is much easier to test, and in some ways much more open to criticism.[44] The same is true of the explanation given by Brunner and Meltzer. In both of these studies the authors identify specific variables to which they believe Fed officials reacted. And in both cases an attempt is made to reinforce their respective positions with an all too casual examination of a small part of the relevant data.

Perhaps one of the biggest faults in Wicker's argument is his failure to mention the credit arrangements between the Fed and other central banks—especially the Bank of England—whose directors wanted to return their nations' currencies to the gold standard. It is extremely important to take these arrangements into account because Wicker's conclusions are based on statements by Strong and other Fed officials regarding the importance to the world economy of a return to the gold standard. If the Fed had no policy tools *other than* open market operations and changes in the discount rate to promote a return to the gold standard, then one might conclude that the international goal dominated open market and discount rate policies. In fact, however, the Fed *did* have another policy tool to employ its efforts to promote a return to gold—direct credit arrangements with foreign central banks.

This does not, of course, preclude the possibility that open market operations and discount rate changes were undertaken for the purpose of achieving the desired international goals. But the failure to recognize means other than these through which the Fed tried to achieve these goals creates the impression that in order to achieve international currency stability, the Fed was limited to direct tampering with the domestic economy.

Stephen V.O. Clarke published a study in 1967 (after Wicker's article and book) entitled *Central Bank Cooperation: 1924-1931* in which he describes *all* of the means known to him by which the Fed (and especially Benjamin Strong) implemented its support for the return to the gold standard.[45] These methods included the extension of loans to foreign banks at the time of their country's return to gold and purchases of foreign exchange to support its value when necessary. This work is important because it strikes a needed balance that frequently appears to be absent from Wicker's study. It is Clarke's contention that the desire of the central bankers to cooperate in reestablishing the gold standard was tempered by (and at times frustrated by) the necessity to achieve certain domestic goals. In Clarke's opinion:

> . . . the maintenance of the international gold standard, however defined, was only one objective among many and one that could not always be easily reconciled with others to which vital importance was attached. In each country the problem that confronted central bankers was essentially the same but took different forms . . . .[O]ften in . . . the United States, . . . the problem appeared in the form of a conflict between the need to ease monetary policy in order to support sterling and the need to tighten it in order to maintain domestic monetary stability.[46]

Specifically, it is Clarke's contention that the Fed cooperated with other central bankers in restoring and maintaining the gold standard in 1924 and 1927. But in 1928-1929, the Fed intensified the problems of England in maintaining the gold standard by pursuing a tight monetary policy in its effort to stop stock market speculation. It is no accident that the Fed cooperated in 1924 and 1927 when the domestic economy was in recession.[47]

Wicker largely restricts his argument to the periods of monetary ease in 1924 and 1927, saying that the reason for this ease was to establish an interest rate differential between New York and London that would reverse the gold flow into the United States.[48] Clarke agrees that the desire to keep rates down in New York, relative to London, was important in the decision to lower the discount rate at the New York Fed and to purchase securities in the last half of 1924 (just prior to Britain's return to gold in April, 1925) and again in the last half of 1927 (when sterling was under considerable pressure).[49] However, Clarke goes on to say that the restrictive policies immediately following these episodes were counter to international goals and forced the Bank of England to restrict credit even further in an already weak British economy. The 1928-1929 episode of credit restriction resulted in "considerable pressure" on sterling.[50]

Clarke also makes it clear that the support of the Fed for sterling was not limited to easing the money market in New York through open market and discount operations. He discusses fully the extent and importance of the credit arrangements between the Fed and the Bank of England at the time of England's return to gold.[51] The Fed also engaged in short-term support by purchases of sterling from time to time.[52]

The impression that Clarke's study conveys is quite different from that of Wicker's, even though the basic theme is the same (the importance of a return to and maintenance of the gold standard). Clarke balances the desire of Strong (and the others) for a return to the gold standard against his desire to maintain domestic stability and his knowledge that the Fed could not ignore domestic problems in the interest of international considerations even if that were his desire. Strong indicated on several occasions that domestic objectives could not be sacrificed to the goal of international stability.[53]

Another interesting idea advanced by Clarke is that the breakdown of international cooperation after the middle of 1928 was the result, in part, of the inability of officials in all countries to understand what was happening in the international economy. He expresses the belief that Strong and Montagu Norman, Governor of the Bank of England during the period in question, could have handled the problems if it were not for their illnesses.[54] This suggests a fourth alternative to the hypotheses regarding Federal Reserve behavior already examined: Federal Reserve policy was inconsistent after 1928 in the pursuit of *international* goals because of the death of Strong. Indeed, Clarke believes that the controversy between Harrison and the Federal Reserve Board after Strong's death was in no small part a conflict between the pursuit of international and domestic goals.[55]

As previously stated, Wicker largely restricts his analysis to the easy money periods of 1924 and 1927. He contends that in 1924 the timing of Federal Reserve purchases of government securities was inconsistent with an anti-recession policy. On his interpretation, the purchases by the Fed between January and June of that year (amounting to $229 million) were *not* expansionary because during the same period their holdings of acceptances declined by $249 million. Wicker attributes the decline in member bank borrowings of over $400 million to the inflow of gold and the return of currency to the banks from circulation, *not* to open market operations.[56] He concludes that, "If the Open Market Investment Committee had deliberately aimed at easing credit by supplying reserves through open-market purchases, it does seem reasonable that they would have compensated for the loss of reserves brought about by a decline in bills bought."[57]

It is unclear exactly how Wicker decided on the appropriate manner in which to "match up" the sources of gains and losses in reserves and to compare the net results with borrowings. Why does he conclude that it was the inflow of gold and the decline in currency outstanding rather than the purchase of government securities that resulted in a decline in borrowings? Is not a policy of purchases of government securities more expansionary than a policy of no purchases or even of sales of securities?

The key seems to be in the fact that the total of the Fed's holdings of government securities and acceptances declined; hence Wicker's comment, cited above, that the expansion in reserves could not have taken place because of open market operations alone (meaning net purchases or sales of government securities and acceptances). This, however, is nonsense.

As Appendix B clearly illustrates, there are strong seasonal components in borrowings, acceptances and currency in circulation. To some extent, Wicker, working with data that is not seasonally adjusted, is probably correct in "matching" the decline in currency in circulation against the decline in borrowings. The change in borrowings in January, 1924, alone was a negative $335 million. In the same month, currency in circulation declined by $395 million. It is no secret that the member banks borrowed in December (as at other times) to provide for an increased demand for currency by the public and then returned those borrowed reserves in January as the currency returned to the banks. The Fed's holdings of acceptances exhibits a similar seasonal pattern.[58] Abstracting from seasonal movements, member bank reserves *did* increase in the first five months of 1924 and member bank borrowings were reduced to an unusually low level.[59] This easing was obviously not damaged by the purchases of government securities and could not have taken place without such purchases. Wicker's argument that these purchases were not expansionary is purely the result of some dubious arithmetic.

After concluding, on the basis described above, that purchases of government securities were *not* expansionary prior to June, 1924, Wicker further concludes that the purchases beginning in June, which *were* expansionary, were not aimed at reviving the economy because "By June . . . both the wholesale price index and the production index had touched bottom."[60] But this argument is questionable on two grounds. One is that Wicker's arithmetic fails to illustrate that purchases of government securities prior to June were not expansionary. The other is that, even if his classifications are correct, it is quite possible that the Fed believed it could do most to promote recovery on the upswing and hesitated to adopt an expansionary policy immediately after a downturn either because of a failure to recognize the turn or because of a fear of overexpansion of credit at the wrong time.[61]

With respect to the easing in 1927, Wicker cites Chandler's conclusion that it was the international situation that was responsible for the decision to ease monetary conditions, without going ". . . over the same ground again."[62] Chandler's conclusion was based not on analysis of the data, but on statements made by Strong and others.[63]

The last incident that Wicker cites as being one in which international considerations were the most important is the raising of the discount rate in 1931 after Britain went off the gold standard and the United States began to lose gold.[64] In this case, it would seem that the contention need not be challenged. Although Friedman and Schwartz express doubts about this episode, most observers agree that such was the case.[65] Such a policy was counter to the needs of the domestic economy.[66]

Like Wicker, Brunner and Meltzer fail to provide any analysis of the data that conclusively supports their explanation of Federal Reserve policy in the period in question. Their conclusions are based partly on policy statements and partly on an analysis of the data that overlooks more than it includes. It can also be argued that Brunner and Meltzer were looking at the wrong variable for the Fed's open market policy instrument.

The primary problem with the empirical analysis of data employed by Brunner and Meltzer is that it is two dimensional when it should be multidimensional. The framework of their analysis simply does not allow for the possibility that the Fed was reacting to variables other than those to which the authors restrict their attention.

Their analysis of the data consists of examining the cumulative first differences in (1) the Federal Reserve Banks' portfolio of government securities and acceptances, (2) the extended monetary base, (3) the Federal Reserve Banks' holdings of government securities, acceptances, and bills discounted, and (4) the interest rate on three to six month Treasury Bills, during the twenty months following the cyclical peaks in May 1923, October 1926, and August 1929.

Brunner and Meltzer note that the purchases and sales of government securities plus acceptances (which they appear to believe is the appropriate variable to represent Federal Reserve open market policy) behaved quite differently in each of the three cycles. From their analysis of the changes in holdings of the sum of government securities, acceptances, *and borrowings*, they conclude that the difference is largely explained by borrowings since the cumulative changes in the sum of all three components display similar patterns in each of the three recessions.[67] Therefore, the differences in the volume of purchases of securities plus acceptances is largely explained by the differences in the volume of borrowings in each recession, or, to quote the authors: "The Riefler-Burgess framework appears to explain the size of open market operations in each of the recessions just as it explains the volume of open market operations in other periods."[68]

From their examination of the cumulative changes in all three of the components of Federal Reserve credit, they notice that purchases of government securities and acceptances failed to offset the decline in bills discounted in any of the recessions. Hence, the changes in Federal Reserve credit ". . . had a deflationary and contractive effect throughout each of the downswings."[69] This was true because ". . . the combined effect was to reduce member bank reserves during each of the three recessions."[70]

In response to their own question, "Why did the Federal Reserve fail to purchase securities or to acquire bills in amounts equal to the decline in member bank borrowing during each of the recessions?"[71] the authors answer that the Fed used short-term interest rates as the "key indicator of monetary policy."[72] And, since their study of the cumulative first differences in short-term rates (on three to six month

Treasury Notes) shows that interest rates fell in each of the recessions, they conclude that the Fed did not fully replace the decline in borrowings with purchases of government securities plus acceptances (thus expanding Federal Reserve credit) because "the key indicator of monetary policy" showed that money was already "easy" and further purchases were therefore unnecessary. This especially explains why the Fed did not purchase more securities and acceptances after the first five months of the Great Depression—interest rates fell precipitously.[73]

The difference between the effectiveness of monetary policy in the two earlier contractions and the Great Depression is explained by the fact that the extended monetary base, the "true" indicator of monetary policy, fell after 1929 whereas it had risen (or not fallen) after the earlier peaks.[74]

Brunner and Meltzer then back up their conclusion drawn from the data with statements from Federal Reserve records that support their interpretation of the reasons for inaction in the Great Depression.[75]

As indicated previously, Brunner and Meltzer's analysis of the data is inadequate for several reasons. One of the most important of these is that they failed to take explicit account of other factors that were changing during the period under analysis. In particular, during the recession of 1923-1924 and 1926-1927, the Fed *was* interested in helping Britain return to the gold standard (in 1923-1924) and remain on the gold standard (in 1926-1927). The problem is, of course, that the two goals (domestic and international) called for the same policy at the same time in each of these two periods. Failure to explicitly recognize the possibility that the Fed was trying to ease monetary conditions for international reasons could easily bias their results: what Brunner and Meltzer attribute to antirecession policy could have been, at least in part, a pro-return-to-gold policy.

Furthermore, their conclusion that the failure of the Fed to expand their holdings of government securities and acceptances in an amount equal to the decline in borrowings had a "deflationary and contractive effect" is simply not warranted. Member bank reserves, from the peak to the trough of the recessions of 1923-1924 and 1926-1927, and during the first twenty months after the peak in 1929, actually *expanded*.[76] To say that monetary policy was deflationary simply because Federal Reserve credit declined is to ignore other very important sources of changes in the member banks' reserve position—a surprising oversight by proponents of the extended monetary base as the key indicator of monetary policy.[77] Federal Reserve officials did not expand their holdings of government securities if other changes in source and uses of reserves made this unnecessary. Again, the failure to explicitly take into account other changes may be responsible for a faulty conclusion.

Furthermore, it is not clear that the officials of the Federal Reserve System thought that their policy should turn expansive immediately after the peak, even assuming that they could recognize the peak at the right time. It is likely that Fed officials felt they should react to help expand credit on the upswing of the cycle while they were not sure that an expansion of credit on the downswing would help to stop the decline. This point will be considered at some length in the next section.

It would appear from the above criticisms that what is necessary for a fuller understanding of Federal Reserve behavior in this period (or any other period for that matter) is an analysis that will explicitly allow for the reaction of the Federal Reserve officials to changes in *all* of the appropriate variables. Multiple regression analysis is employed in Chapter Three in an attempt to hold "other things the same" statistically in order to avoid attributing a change in policy to the wrong variable. It is a proven principle of econometric analysis that the omission of variables that are correlated with one or more of the included variables will "bias" the results. This is what *could* have biased Brunner and Meltzer's results even though they were not obtained from regression analysis; the principle is the same.

Finally, Brunner and Meltzer use purchases and sales of acceptances and government securities as the open market policy instrument. It is extremely doubtful that this is a proper procedure. While it is true that purchases and sales of government securities and of acceptances have the same effect on reserves (ceteris paribus), and that the transactions are similar in nature (both involving the purchase of financial paper), they are also different inasmuch as the purchases and sales of government securities were undertaken at the initiative of the Fed while purchases of acceptances were undertaken at the initiative of member banks. Once purchased, acceptances were then held until they matured, whereas government securities were bought *and sold* in the open market to effect Federal Reserve policy.[78]

It is true that there were times when Federal Reserve officials would express the desire to ease credit through the purchase of acceptances rather than government securities, probably as a result of the real bills doctrine.[79] But for the most part, the control exercised by the Reserve Banks over the volume of acceptances they held was control through the setting of the rate at which they would purchase acceptances. The policy toward government securities was just the opposite—the System bought or sold these securities at the going open market rate in a volume designed to affect member bank credit.[80]

In addition, there is strong evidence from the spectral analysis presented in Appendix B (and from the account of Charles O. Hardy[81]) that member banks used acceptances in response to seasonal needs while the purchase and sale of government securities exhibits primarily a cyclical variation. This would seem to indicate that the purchase and sales of government securities was the policy instrument used by the Fed. To use the sum of the two would confuse the issue.

Therefore, in the statistical work in Chapter Three, the open market policy instrument used is the purchase and sale of government securities. But the buying rate on acceptances and the discount rate (both at the New York Reserve Bank) are also explained as part of the model.

Finally, the procedure used by Brunner and Meltzer of looking only at the policy of the Fed during recessions ignores the question of policy during recovery. By default, their method cannot explain the actions taken by the Fed during periods of expansion. While the main question may well be one of recession policy, and as stated before, especially the question of policy after the peak in 1929, Federal Reserve policy during expansionary periods is also of interest. Indeed, the problems of recessions may well be influenced by monetary policy prior to the peak.

It may be said, in conclusion, that in spite of their limitations, each of the explanations criticized above has some merit, and each has provided additional hypotheses to be tested. But none of the authors has attempted a thorough test of the relevant hypothesis. Each of the explanations has merit, but each should be tested against the data if at all possible.

More on Federal Reserve Policy

The works described so far are all based on a myriad of primary sources which, as previously noted, have led the authors to differing conclusions. The purpose of this section is to add to the explanations given by Wicker and the others additional information from a variety of sources. While there has been no attempt to cover the entire collection of primary sources used by these authors in their studies, *some* of the same sources have been explored in an attempt to provide a fuller description of Federal Reserve thinking where that has seemed necessary. In addition, a summary volume of the records of the Federal Reserve Board and Open Market Investment Committee (OMIC) for the years 1923 to mid-1931[82] has been examined in order to get a feeling for the information discussed by the decision makers in this period and to attempt to discover what variables should be used in the statistical tests in Chapter Three.

The problem of providing sufficient credit to promote the production and consumption of maximum output without encouraging a speculative buildup of inventories was identified as *the* problem of credit control. As Friedman and Schwartz have observed, this idea gradually evolved into an inventory theory of the business cycle and is intimately related to the real bills doctrine.[86] Credit must be of just such a quantity and quality that it provides for legitimate business needs without encouraging speculation. Before 1928, speculation referred to speculation in commodities in anticipation of commodity price increases, not to speculation in the stock market.[87]

Federal Reserve officials apparently saw price increases as being *healthy* for the economy by calling forth a greater supply of output. This is why they did not find price increases per se objectionable. They did fear, however, that price increases might encourage businessmen to speculate in inventories. This buildup of inventories could then be responsible for a later decline in output. The theory is never fully explained, but this is apparently the reasoning behind the emphasis on providing sufficient credit to promote output and consumption but *not* inventory speculation.

Officials of the Federal Reserve System were always opposed to any suggestion that it was their duty to provide for stable prices.[88] The reason for this opposition is probably revealed in the observation in the *Tenth Annual Report* (published in 1924) that *some* price increases are probably inevitable, and perhaps desirable, as long as output is also increasing.[89] There is no indication that Federal Reserve officials were interested in price stabilization, per se, as a policy goal.

It is difficult to discern from the *Tenth Annual Report* whether the Board really believed that they should attempt to combat a recession or not. Indeed, at times it sounds as if they were proposing a procyclical policy: "The Federal Reserve supplies the needed additions to credit in times of business expansion and takes up the slack in times of business recession."[90] There is nowhere in the report any indication that Federal Reserve policy was or should have been geared to stopping a downturn. Rather, it appears that the Fed attempted to restrain the economy as it approached full employment and aid recovery with credit expansion:

> It seems clear that if business is undergoing a rapid expansion and is in danger of developing an unhealthy or speculative boom, it should not be assisted by too easy credit conditions . . . . It seems equally obvious that if industry and trade are in process of recovery after a period of reaction, they should be given the support and encouragement of cheaper credit by the prompt establishment at the Federal Reserve banks of rates that will invite the use of Federal Reserve credit to facilitate business recovery.[91]

The failure of the Federal Reserve System to implement a more expansionary policy following soon after the peaks of 1923 and 1926 documented by Wicker[92] may well be testimony to the serious doubt about the efficacy of easy money policies during a downswing, although Wicker interprets the timing differently.[93] It seems likely that Federal Reserve officials hesitated to expand credit too rapidly immediately after a peak for fear of stimulating speculation. According to the theory expounded in the *Tenth Annual Report* and summarized above, credit expansion at full employment could only result in price increases and commodity speculation.

It is important to note, however, that Burgess, in his study published in 1927, describes the countercyclical nature of Federal

Reserve policy. It cannot, therefore, be concluded that the Federal Reserve officials believed that their policy should be procyclical, although this is how many people have interpreted their role.

The importance of international considerations is not overlooked in the *Tenth Annual Report.* In reference to the large gold holdings of the United States and the Federal Reserve Banks, the Board stated that, "It is the part of prudence . . . to pursue a course which will enable them [the Reserve Banks] to part with such portion of this gold as Europe will need to reclaim for currency restoration with a minimum of inconvenience and disturbance to our internal financial and economic situation."[95] But the larger part of the report is concerned with domestic affairs. That international motives were stressed elsewhere, however, has been amply documented by Wicker, Chandler, and Clarke.[96]

The emphasis given to the prevention of commodity speculation in the *Tenth Annual Report* changed to an emphasis on stock market speculation in late 1927 and early 1928. Until then, the Federal Reserve System had largely refused to consider itself responsible for controlling stock market speculation.[97] In 1928 and 1929, however, that attitude changed; and there can be little doubt that it was the purpose of Federal Reserve officials to stop stock market speculation in 1928 and 1929. No one really disagrees that this was the reason behind the restrictive policy adopted in 1928 and extended into 1929.

The expansionary policy of 1927 was undertaken, either for domestic or international reasons, or both, with full knowledge that such a policy might increase speculation in the stock market.[98] Indeed, the Federal Reserve System has been accused of feeding the speculation with their 1927 policy.[99]

There can be little doubt, however, that the restrictive policy adopted in 1928 was intended to stop speculation on the stock market.[100] But this, too, is subjected to the statistical tests in Chapter Three.

The cyclical peak came in August, 1929, and Federal Reserve policy changed from restrictive to expansionary soon after. This time the New York Reserve Bank, with George Harrison as president, led the way in October with purchases of government securities not authorized by the Board. This initial response would appear to have been to the decline in the stock market, and not to the decline in business. This was the last time that Harrison challenged the leadership of the Board in any significant manner.[101]

A reading of the summary of the minutes of the Open Market Investment Committee (OMIC) for the years 1928 and 1929 provides some interesting insights into the thinking of Federal Reserve officials during this period.

One of the points that is clear from the summary is the conflict between the New York Reserve Bank and the Board over the appropriate policy in 1929—whether the discount rate should be raised or the Board's policy of "direct action" should be pursued.[102] Friedman and Schwartz have carefully documented this conflict;[103] and, as previously noted, Clarke has extended the analysis to attempt to show that the conflict included the question of priorities assigned to international versus domestic goals. It was at this time, according to Clarke, that international cooperation fell apart.[104]

The minutes of the meeting of the OMIC for July 18, 1928, contain the interesting observation that "If the present high interest rates are continued for several months, it seems probable that business activity may be affected six months or a year from now."[105] This is an interesting prediction considering the turn of events a year later.

The idea expressed was apparently based on the belief that high interest rates discouraged new construction activity.[106] Nevertheless, an easier policy was not suggested until September, 1929.[107] However, a letter from Harrison to the Board in April of that year suggested that discount rates should be *raised* to hasten the day when a return to an easier money policy could be realized. The reason for his concern was the inflow of gold, which was ". . . another evidence of the continued pressure upon foreign exchange caused by the strain of high rates in this country . . . ." Harrison went on to point out that this could possibly have disastrous effects on the gold standard.[108] Of course, it is a matter of history that the Board continued to refuse to permit an increase in the New York discount rate.[109]

The summary of the minutes from the time of the stock market crash until the end of the summary in mid-1931 provides some insight into the reasons for inaction on the part of the System.[110] To a large extent, the summary tends to support the conclusions of Brunner and Meltzer (previously noted) that the members hesitated to act further because of a belief that credit was already "easy" and because of serious doubt by many members of the efficacy of further easing in preventing the continued decline in business.[111] From March, 1930, on, the opinion of the majority of members of both the Board and the Open Market Policy Conference (newly formed in that year) seems to have been that a further easing of credit conditions would make credit "too easy" and could result in speculation.[112]

However, it is evident from the minutes that the decline in interest rates was not considered to be simply the result of an easing from the supply side. It was fully recognized that the declining rates were also the result of decreasing demand for credit.[113] This is an important point and one which Brunner and Meltzer failed to express. The conclusion cannot, therefore, be that the System officials took the decline in interest rates to be the result of easing from the supply side alone.

There is also some indication that the hesitancy in the first half of 1930 was due, at least in part, to a fear of reviving stock market speculation. It was not until June, 1930, that Harrison told the Executive Committee that he saw no danger of reviving speculation.[114] Friedman and Schwartz have also found evidence that this may have been one of the reasons for hesitancy by the System.[115]

From June on, the minutes reflect the controversy within the Fed regarding the possible influence of credit policy on the bond market. Harrison tried to sell the System on the idea that further easing would eventually affect the bond market and long term rates. This, in turn, would revive business interest in capital expenditures.[116] Other members expressed doubt, however, that the Fed's policy could correct what was essentially a problem of overproduction and excess capacity.[117]

Federal Reserve policy continued largely unchanged until September, 1931, when an increase in the discount rate was put into effect, presumably in response to Britain's departure from gold and the resulting large outflow of gold from the United States. This policy was, of course, opposite to the needs of the domestic economy; and therefore there has been little doubt that it was inspired by international considerations.[118]

The most significant change in Federal Reserve policy after September, 1931, came in 1932 when the System began large-scale purchases of government securities, ostensibly in response to the Glass-Stegall Act, which permitted the use of government securities as backing for Federal Reserve Notes.[119] Friedman and Schwartz attribute the change in policy more to Congressional pressure, however.[120]

Summary

This chapter has defined three different hypotheses regarding Federal Reserve behavior in the period 1923-1931. Additional information has been provided in an attempt to fill in some of the missing pieces that are believed to be most important to an understanding of the thinking of Federal Reserve policy makers in this period.

The basic conclusions from this chapter may be summarized very briefly before going on to a specific formulation and testing of the hypothesis in Chapter Three. These conclusions are based on all the works described in this chapter, and reflect only the policy statements of the officials. The evidence provided by the statistical analysis in Chapter Three is summarized at the end of that chapter and the conflicts between statements and actions are then brought into focus.

Based on the evidence of the present chapter, it is reasonable to believe that Federal Reserve policy prior to 1928 was influenced by the desire to achieve *both* domestic and international goals. In particular, the primary domestic goal was to provide for the needs of production, distribution, and consumption without encouraging commodity speculation. The primary international goal was to promote a return to and a continuation of the gold standard throughout the world. It is difficult to say which was *more* important since they largely coincided during this period.

After 1928, the primary domestic goal was the restriction of speculation on the stock market. While the international goal likely remained the same as before, it would appear to have been relegated to a secondary position since the policy adopted after that time was detrimental to the continuation of the gold standard in Europe.

From the collapse of the stock market in October, 1929, until September, 1931, the primary objective of the Federal Reserve System seems to have been the promotion of recovery through an easier money policy. However, this policy was not pursued to its fullest possible extent, probably because of the belief that money was already "easy" and because of the belief of some of the officials of the Fed that further easing could not promote recovery and might even be detrimental.

In September, 1931, apparently in response to Britain's departure from the gold standard and the subsequent outflow of gold from the United States, the Fed raised discount and acceptance rates. In this case, the goal of domestic recovery was subjugated to the preservation of the United States' gold stock.

NOTES

1. Chandler, *Benjamin Stone*, p. 3

2. Friedman and Schwartz, *Monetary History*, p. 411.

3. Ibid., see especially pp. 362-391.

4. Ibid., pp. 407-419.

5. Ibid., p. 351.

6. Wicker, "A Reinterpretation," p. 327.

7. Ibid., pp. 329-337.

8. Ibid., p. 333.

9. Ibid., p. 337.

10. Ibid., pp. 326 and 329-33. See especially Wicker's quoting of Strong's views on p. 330.

11. In his book *Federal Reserve Monetary Policy* Wicker devotes considerable time to the analysis of all of the factors influencing the decisions of the policy makers as recorded in public and private statements.

12. Wicker, "A Reinterpretation," pp. 339-342.

13. Brunner and Meltzer, "What Did We Learn?," pp. 334-348.

14. Ibid., pp. 339-340. This is, of course, the same theory of open market operations set forth by Wicker under the name of the Burgess-Strong doctrine.

15. Ibid., pp. 339-343.

16. Ibid. "The extended monetary base equals total reserves plus currency issued by the Federal Reserve and the Treasury adjusted for changes in reserve requirements resulting from policy decisions and redistribution of deposits between classes of banks and types of deposit." Ibid., p. 336, n. 6.

17. Ibid., p. 341.

18. Brunner and Meltzer refer to this explanation as the Riefler-Burgess doctrine ("What Did We Learn?" pp. 339-340). Wicker calls it the Burgess-Strong or the Burgess-Strong-Riefler doctrine ("A Reinterpretation," pp. 329-332). The discussion by Friedman and Schwartz omits specific reference to the doctrine, but its presence is implicit in their discussion (*Monetary History*, pp. 251-254).

19. W. Randolph Burgess, *The Reserve Banks and the Money Market* (New York: Harper and Brothers Publishers, 1927), pp. 214-215. See also pp. 182-184 for a discussion of the "tradition against borrowing."

20. Brunner and Meltzer, "What Did We Learn?" pp. 339-343. Friedman and Schwartz, *Monetary History*, p. 269.

21. Wicker, "A Reinterpretation," pp. 326-327.

22. Brunner and Meltzer, "What Did We Learn?" p. 338. Wicker, "A Reinterpretation," p. 326. Friedman and Schwartz, *Monetary History*, pp. 407-419.

23. See particularly Wicker, "A Reinterpretation," pp. 332-335.

24. Brunner and Meltzer, "What Did We Learn?" pp. 337-343.

25. Friedman and Schwartz, *Monetary History*, p. 411.

26. Wicker, "A Reinterpretation," pp. 327-328.

27. Brunner and Meltzer, "What Did We Learn?" pp. 337-338.

28. Friedman and Schwartz, *Monetary History*, p. 407.

29. Ibid., p. 408.

30. Ibid., pp. 412-413.

31. Wicker explicitly refers to the Friedman-Schwartz hypothesis as alleging inconsistent behavior. (Wicker, "A Reinterpretation," p. 327.) Brunner and Meltzer contrast their hypothesis of ". . . a single, consistent framework, . . ." with the Friedman-Schwartz hypothesis. (Brunner and Meltzer, "What Did We Learn?" p. 338.)

I am grateful to Professor Rendigs Fels for pointing out the failure of an earlier draft of this thesis to clarify this problem of terminology.

32. Brunner and Meltzer, "What Did We Learn?" see especially pp. 337-345 and the charts used as supporting evidence.

33. Wicker, "A Reinterpretation," see especially pp. 332-337.

34. Friedman and Schwartz, *Monetary History*, pp. 409-411.

35. Ibid., p. 419.

36. Chandler, *Benjamin Strong*, pp. 27-30.

37. Friedman and Schwartz, *Monetary History*, pp. 410-411.

38. Ibid., pp. 412-413.

39. Chandler, *Benjamin Strong*, pp. 423ff.

40. Ibid., pp. 454-455.

41. Ibid., p. 460, quoting from a letter by Strong to Walter Stewart, August 3, 1928.

42. Friedman and Schwartz, *Monetary History*, p. 289, n. 69.

43. Wicker points out that Strong would have faced a powerful opposition from the majority of members of the Executive Committee of the Open Market Policy Conference (the latter being newly formed to include all of the governors of the Federal Reserve Banks in 1930) even if he had lived. Wicker, "A Reinterpretation," pp. 329-331. This does not, however, preclude the possibility that Strong would have led the New York Reserve Bank to a policy of its own.

44. The criticism of Wicker's theory that follows is based on his article ("A Reinterpretation") since this contains the most concise statement of his explanation. It should be noted, however, that his book *(Federal Reserve Monetary Policy, 1917-1933)*, which was published a year after the appearance of his article, contains a more rigorous examination of Federal Reserve policy in the period in question. Nevertheless, the conclusions are the same and hence the criticisms that follow may be applied to his more thorough study as well.

45. Stephen V.O. Clarke, *Central Bank Cooperation: 1924-1931* (New York: Federal Reserve Bank of New York, 1967).

46. Ibid., p. 30.

47. Ibid., pp. 42-43, 85-96, 124-127, 147-168.

48. Wicker, "A Reinterpretation," pp. 332-337.

49. Clarke, *Central Bank Corporation*, pp. 85-86, 124-126.

50. Ibid., pp. 88-89, 147-150.

51. Ibid., pp. 81-85.

52. Ibid., pp. 174-176.

53. Ibid., pp. 80, 98, 106. Clarke also provides considerable coverage of Strong's objections to any international organization of central bankers to promote international goals on the grounds of not wanting to sacrifice control over the domestic economy. (Ibid., pp. 36-40.)

54. Ibid., pp. 141-142.

55. Ibid., pp. 151-160.

56. Wicker, "A Reinterpretation," pp. 333-334.

57. Ibid., p. 333.

58. See, for example, Burgess, *Federal Reserve Policy and Benjamin Strong*, pp. 289-293.

59. Average daily reserves of member banks were $1,922 million in May, 1924. This compares with a figure of $1,874 million for May, 1923. Average daily holdings of discounted bills (by the Federal Reserve banks) was $433 million in May, 1924—one of the lowest levels reached in the period under examination.

60. Wicker, "A Reinterpretation," p. 334.

61. See below for a fuller explanation of this point.

62. Wicker, "A Reinterpretation," p. 336.

63. Chandler, *Benjamin Strong*, pp. 438-447.

64. Wicker, "A Reinterpretation," pp. 336-337.

65. Friedman and Schwartz, *Monetary History*, pp. 399-406.

66. For Brunner and Meltzer's criticisms of Wicker, see their "What Did We Learn?" pp. 335-337.

67. Ibid., pp. 339-341.

68. Ibid., p. 341.

69. Ibid.

70. Ibid., p. 340

71. Ibid., p. 341.

72 Ibid., pp. 341-343.

73. Ibid.

74. Ibid., pp. 338, 345.

75. Ibid., pp. 346-347.

76. From the peak in May, 1923, to the trough in July, 1924, average daily reserves of member banks expanded from $1,874 million to $2,046 million. The same figures for the peak in October, 1926, and trough in November, 1927, are $2,219 million and $2,373 million. Finally, in the twenty-month period after the peak in August, 1929, reserves expanded from $2,322 million to $2,376 million (in April, 1931). See U.S. Board of Governors of the Federal Reserve System, *Banking and Monetary Statistics* (Washington, D.C.: U.S. Board of Governors, 1943), pp. 369-371.

77. The authors do take these other changes into account later in their paper. (See Brunner and Meltzer, "What Did We Learn?" pp. 344-346). Their point is that if other things had been the same, the effect of the change in Federal Reserve Credit would have been to reduce reserves. But the point being made in the text is that other things did *not* remain the same and therefore the total effect of changes in all sources and uses of reserves was to expand reserves. Federal Reserve Credit might have expanded if other things had remained the same. A more complete analysis is necessary for a clearer understanding.

78. See, for example, U.S. Federal Reserve Board, *Tenth Annual Report* (Washington, D.C.: U.S. Government Printing Office, 1924), pp. 11-16, for a discussion of the similarities between purchases and sales of government securities and acceptances. But see also Burgess, *Federal Reserve Policy and Benjamin Strong*, pp. 140-143 and 206-213, and Hardy, *Credit Policies*, pp. 27-28, for the careful distinction between the two.

The statements in the text require some modification. The Federal Reserve Banks purchased most of their acceptances directly from the member banks at the initiative of the latter. These bills were held to maturity. However, the Reserve Banks also stood ready to buy from bill dealers under a resale agreement whereby the dealer would buy back the bills within fifteen days. (See Burgess, *Federal Reserve Policy and Benjamin Strong*, pp. 140-143.

It is also true that the Reserve Banks purchased government securities in small amounts directly from dealers under a similar resale agreement. Here, the initiative was the dealer's and the securities were sold back to the dealer within fifteen days. (Burgess, *Federal Reserve Policy and Benjamin Strong*, pp. 208-209.)

79. Friedman and Schwartz, *Monetary History*, pp. 266-268.

80. Burgess, *Federal Reserve Policy and Benjamin Strong*, pp. 206-213. Hardy, *Credit Policies*, pp. 248-249.

81. Hardy, *Credit Policies*, p. 28.

82. This volume (actually, the summary is divided into two continuous volumes) was edited by Winfield W. Riefler, Secretary of the Federal Open Market Committee, in February, 1956. However, it was not placed in the library of the Board of Governors of the Federal Reserve System and made available to the public until April, 1971. Mr. Riefler described the volume as follows:

> The record of discussions and policy decisions relating to the operations of the Federal Open Market Investment Committee during the years 1923-30, and of the Open

> Market Policy Conference during 1930 and the first half of 1931, has been re-examined recently. In the belief that this record may have a continuing reference value to present and future members of the Federal Open Market Committee, the parts describing actions taken and the reasons for those actions have been reproduced. The parts omitted consist largely of the routine reports which do not seem essential to an adequate historical review of Committee operations in those years.

U.S. Board of Governors, *Open Market Investment Policy: Excerpts, 1923-1928 and 1928-Mid-1931* (Washington, DC: U.S. Board of Governors of the Federal Reserve System, 1956). This summary volume will hereafter be referred to as *Excerpts.*

83. U.S. Federal Reserve Board, *Tenth Annual Report* (Washington, DC: U.S. Government Printing Office, 1924).

84. Ibid., pp. 34-35.

85. Ibid., p. 5. Compare Wicker's similar conclusion in "A Reinterpretation," pp. 341-342. He there cites additional references that support this interpretation.

86. Friedman and Schwartz, *Monetary History*, p. 253.

87. See Hardy's discussion of this in *Credit Policies*, pp. 74-82.

88. Ibid., pp. 74-82 and 199-226. *Tenth Annual Report*, pp. 31-32.

89. *Tenth Annual Report*, pp. 5, 34-35.

90. Ibid., p. 10.

91. Ibid.

92. Wicker, "A Reinterpretation," pp. 333-336. A fuller documentation is provided in his *Federal Reserve Monetary Policy, 1917-1933*, pp. 77-94, 106-116.

93. Hardy, an outside observer, also expressed doubt about the usefulness of Federal Reserve policy in stopping a downswing, or, for that matter, promoting recovery. *Credit Policies*, pp. 88-90.

94. Burgess, *Federal Reserve Policy and Benjamin Strong*, pp. 196-198. Friedman and Schwartz believe that the "procyclical" theory espoused in the *Tenth Annual Report* was not an important part of Reserve thinking. Rather, this idea was the result of a confusion between the appropriate responses to seasonal versus cyclical movements. Federal Reserve Credit was "proseasonal" but "anticyclical." *Monetary History*, pp. 294-296.

95. *Tenth Annual Report*, p. 20.

96. Wicker, *Federal Reserve Monetary Policy, 1917-1933;* Chandler, *Benjamin Strong;* Clarke, *Central Bank Corporation.*

97. Hardy, *Credit Policies*, pp. 118-128.

98. Memorandum from Strong to Board, November 2, 1927 in *Excerpts*, p. 147.

The minutes of the joint meeting of the Board and the Open Market Investment Committee of July 27, 1927, contain this note:

> The most important consideration at the meeting was undoubtedly the fact that the differential between the rates in New York and the rates in London was not sufficient to enable London, and therefore the rest of Europe, to avoid general advances in rates this autumn unless rates here were lowered, and that the consequences of such high rates as would result in Europe would be unfavorable to the marketing of our export produce aboard and would have an adverse effect generally on world trade.

From *Excerpts*, p. 130. This statement was cited by Wicker ("A Reinterpretation," p. 336) as conclusive proof of the international objectives behind the easy-money policy of 1927.

99. See, for example, Adolph C. Miller, "Responsibility for Federal Reserve Policies: 1927-1929, " *American Economic Review*, XXV (September, 1935), pp. 442-458. Interestingly, Miller blames the New York Reserve Bank for initiating the policy of 1927 (ibid., p. 442). This would seem to further support the Friedman-Schwartz hypothesis.

100. *Excerpts*, pp. 177-289. U.S. Federal Reserve Board, *Fifteenth Annual Report* (Washington, DC: U.S. Government Printing Office, 1929), pp. 1-7. U.S. Federal Reserve Board, *Sixteenth Annual Report* (Washington, DC: U.S. Government Printing Office, 1930), pp. 1-4.

101. Friedman and Schwartz, *Monetary History*, pp. 362-368.

102. *Excerpts*, pp. 264-348.

103. Friedman and Schwartz, *Monetary History*, pp. 361-380.

104. Clarke, *Central Bank Corporation*, pp. 144-171.

105. Memorandum of Acting Chairman, July 18, 1928, in *Excerpts*, p. 218.

106. Ibid.

107. Preliminary Memorandum of Chairman, September 24, 1929, in *Excerpts*, p. 348.

108. Letter of Harrison to Board, April 11, 1929, in *Excerpts*, p. 294.

109. The reply of the Board came in a meeting on April 24, 1929. Harrison

> . . . was advised of the opinion of a majority of the Board that approval of an increase in discount rates would be confession of the inability of the System to deal with a limited number of member banks who are misusing its facilities other than by imposing the penalty of increased rates upon the entire banking and business structure of the country.

Excerpts. p. 300.

110. *Excerpts*, pp. 350-387.

111. Brunner and Meltzer, "What Did We Learn?" pp. 345-348. This support is not surprising since it was from the minutes that these authors obtained their explanation.

112. *Excerpts*, pp. 414ff.

113. Preliminary memorandum of Secretary of OMIC, March 24, 1930, in *Excerpts*, p. 420.

114. *Excerpts*, p. 472.

115. Friedman and Schwartz, *Monetary History*, p. 375, n. 103.

116. *Excerpts*, pp. 471-509.

117. Ibid., pp. 501-506. Governor Norris was a leading proponent of this idea. See also Clay J. Anderson, *A Half-Century of Federal Reserve Policymaking*, 1914-1964 (Philadelphia: Federal Reserve Bank of Philadelphia, 1956), pp. 62-64.

118. For an account of the traditional explanation, and the authors' rejection of that explanation, see Friedman and Schwartz, *Monetary History*, pp. 381-383, 400-406. See also U.S. Federal Reserve Board, *Eighteenth Annual Report* (Washington, DC: U.S. Government Printing Office, 1932), pp. 6-7.

119. U.S. Federal Reserve Board, *Nineteenth Annual Report* (Washington, DC: U.S. Government Printing Office, 1933), pp. 16-19.

120. Friedman and Schwartz, *Monetary History*, pp. 384-406.

CHAPTER THREE

Federal Reserve Behavior: Quantification and Testing

The present chapter is devoted to a formal statement of the hypotheses to be tested, a quantification of the hypothesis in two different but similar models, and the testing of these models against the data. The approach to be used is described in the first section, the derivations of the models follow, and the conclusions drawn from the testing are summarized at the end of the chapter.

The Assumption of a Disutility Function

The approach used below in formulating a concise statement of Federal Reserve behavior assumes that the policymakers acted as though they were trying to minimize a disutility function in which their disutility is a positive function of the differences between the actual and desired values of certain target variables. The minimization process is constrained by a set of equations assumed to describe the Fed's view of the operation of the economy.[1]

The disutility function is assumed to be quadratic, and the constraints are assumed to be linear.[2] The variables entering the disutility function are, in the first model, the variables by which the Fed hopes to influence the economy. In the second model, the variables are the assumed ultimate target variables. The difference between these two approaches will become clear later in the development of this chapter.

The nature of the quadratic disutility function is such that the disutility of the policy maker is increased in proportion to the square of the difference between the actual and desired values of certain target variables. In addition, the use of squared differences between actual and desired values means that obtaining a value of the target variable that is above the desired value is equally as bad as obtaining a value that is below the desired value. Therefore it may be useful to assume that certain target variables are without an upper (or a lower) desired value, i.e., that the Fed officials desire to make some variables as great (or as small) as possible.[3]

The two models make use of the two alternative disutility functions, but in each case the equations for the policy variables are derived by minimizing the disutility function subject to the constraints imposed by the Fed's assumed model of the economy. The equations are then tested against the data.

Ideally, after fitting the regressions, it would be possible to discover the weights (in the disutility function) attached to the achievement of each of the goals, domestic and international, and thus determine which of the goals were the most important. However, as Wood has explained, it is impossible to retrieve from the final results the coefficients entering the disutility function (i.e., the weights). This problem is inherent in the approach.[4] Therefore, the conclusions are based on the coefficients of the reduced form equations.

Finally, in order to test the Friedman-Schwartz hypothesis of inconsistency, the period is divided into two parts and regressions run for each subperiod. The results provide some evidence on the theory of inconsistent behavior.

The Two Models: An Overview

It is possible to classify the variables used in the present analysis into four groups: policy variables, intermediate variables, money market indicators, and target variables.[5] The policy variables used in this study are purchases and sales of government securities, the discount rate at the New York Reserve Bank, and the buying rate on bankers' acceptances at the New York Reserve Bank. The intermediate variable through which the Fed believed it affected the economy is member bank borrowings (based on the Riefler-Burgess doctrine). The indicators of money market conditions are taken to be short-term open market interest rates and the volume of member bank credit outstanding. Finally, the ultimate target variables are output, speculation (in commodities and in the stock market), and gold flows.

The analysis is developed in greater detail later in the chapter; but for the present it may simply be said that the Fed used its policy variables to affect member bank borrowings directly, the cost and volume of bank credit directly and indirectly through the effects on borrowings (which in turn affected the market for short-term credit), and the target variables indirectly through the effects on the market for short-term credit.

In the first model it is assumed that the variables entering the disutility function of the Federal Reserve policy makers are the indicators of money market conditions. The second model is built around a disutility function that includes the ultimate target variables and is therefore more complex. As will be seen, there are reasons for preferring each of these models.

Both models have in common a basic submodel of the money market based on the Riefler-Burgess doctrine and a theory of the demand for credit implicit in the literature. The second common element of the two models is the equation that describes the behavior of member banks in borrowing at the Reserve Banks.

Under the Riefler-Burgess doctrine, the supply of short-term credit is a negative function of member bank indebtedness and the discount rate. In other words, the supply of credit is negatively related to the cost and volume of borrowing from the Federal Reserve System. It is probably also true that the officials of the Fed thought of the acceptance rate as having a negative influence on the supply of short-term credit since this rate, like the discount rate, was a cost to member banks of obtaining needed reserves. Finally, the supply of credit is a positive function of the interest rate.

Short-term credit was thought to be used by borrowers for three main purposes: to finance the flow of goods from production to consumption (i.e., to "finance trade"), to finance the speculative buildup of commodity stocks, and to finance speculation in the stock market. Of course, the Fed viewed only the first of these as a "legitimate" use of credit.

Therefore, the demand for credit is a positive function of output, commodity speculation, and stock market speculation. It is also, of course, a negative function of the interest rate.

Again according to the Riefler-Burgess doctrine, member banks borrowed primarily because of the need to replenish reserves. Therefore, member bank borrowing is first and foremost a function of "need." However, it was also accepted by some of the officials that the discount rate had a negative effect on borrowing, although with a lag.[6] It is also likely that the buying rate on acceptances affected the volume of member bank borrowing in a positive way since selling acceptances to the Fed is an alternative means of raising needed reserves. The higher the acceptance rate, the greater the incentive to borrow needed reserves. If it could be argued that banks at times borrowed, or at least stayed in debt, because it was profitable to do so, then the interest rate at which they could lend would also enter the relationship. However, the strong view to the contrary held by most System officials (i.e., that banks did not borrow for profit), makes it unlikely that they thought borrowings would vary positively with the short-term rate of interest. Hence, this rate is excluded from the borrowings function.

These are the two common elements of the models developed below, and their exact specification is given in the formulations of the next two sections.

Model I: The Short-Term Money Market as the Goal

In this formulation, it is assumed that Federal Reserve Officials were content simply to manipulate the cost and volume of short-term credit, that is, that the variables entering their disutility function were the indicators of short-term credit conditions. The implicit assumption is that Federal Reserve officials believed that once they had affected the terms on which credit was available, they could do no more. Therefore, they simply aimed for the indicators of the conditions of the short-term credit market assuming that if they achieved the "right" amount of ease, then output, speculation, and gold flows would adjust to their desired levels.

This approach might be labeled "shortsighted." Instead of thinking in terms of ultimate goals, it is assumed that the officials were not explicitly looking beyond the short-term credit market. Instead of judging their success or failure by the values achieved for the ultimate target variables, they were satisfied simply to affect the indicators of the conditions of the market for short-term credit.

These indicators, as described above, are the rate of interest (the cost of credit) and the volume of credit. It would, however, be superfluous to include both the cost and the volume of credit because both are derived from the same model of the short-term credit market. A statement of the disutility function in terms of one would be the same as a statement in terms of the other. Therefore, the cost of short-term credit is chosen in this model as *the* variable that the Fed chose to try to adjust in its efforts to achieve its ultimate domestic and international goals.

This formulation is appealing for its simplicity. There is good reason to believe that Federal Reserve officials did not have any clear idea of how their efforts were ultimately connected with the target variables. They clearly stated how they thought their actions affected short-term interest rates, but they had only vague ideas as to how the short-term rates in turn affected the economy. Burgess makes this clear in his explanation of Federal Reserve policy.[7] He also emphasizes the importance of short-term credit:

> To the extent that the Reserve System exercises an influence upon social welfare in this country it does so by insuring a supply of credit adapted to the needs of the people. And interest rates are perhaps the best available measure of the adaptation of the credit supply to the country's needs.
>
> Interest rates are interesting primarily not as the price we pay for money, but as indicators of credit conditions.[8]

Certainly this information is consistent with Brunner and Meltzer's theory of Federal Reserve behavior.[9] And it is also consistent with

Wicker's theory since he concludes that the Fed was attempting primarily to affect member bank borrowing through its open market operations.[10] Since the rate of interest is a function of borrowings, and since open market operations are designed to affect borrowings because of the desire to affect interest rates, it makes little difference whether the disutility function is expressed in terms of borrowings or in terms of the interest rate.[11]

The disutility function can therefore be stated very simply as:

$$d_t = w_1 (r_t - r_t^*)^2 \qquad (I.1)$$

where d_t = the disutility in time t attached to missing the goal

r_t = the actual short-term rate of interest in time t

r_t^* = the desired short-term rate of interest rate in time t

w_1 = the weight attached to achieving the goal

This disutility function can be altered slightly to allow for the probability that System officials preferred *not* to engage in open market operations. Wood took this approach on the grounds that "The ordinary bureaucratic preference for doing nothing, rather than risking a wrong action, is sufficient . . ." to warrant the inclusion of open market purchases and sales as a variable adding to the disutility of the policy makers.[12]

The same reasoning as used by Wood is probably even more relevant here. This was a period during which Federal Reserve officials were very unsure of their influence on the economy. They had a theory; but, as indicated by Burgess,[13] they were not at all certain of their exact effects on the ultimate target variables. This could easily lead to hesitancy in acting; they might well prefer inaction except when the situation clearly called for action. The controversy referred to in Chapter Two over the appropriate policy in 1930 and 1931 would seem to testify to this point.

Moreover, the Fed was then, as now, subject to constant criticism by outsiders. Congressional hearings were held on bills that would have legislated how the Fed should handle its policy.[14] The relatively new System was undoubtedly particularly sensitive to this criticism. This would surely add to their preference for no action since they could not then be accused of "meddling."

The same can be said of changing the discount and acceptance rates. The Fed was aware of the psychological influence of changing these rates, particularly the discount rate,[15] and might therefore have hesitated to enact such changes.

Allowing for the possibility that the System preferred not to change policy, equation (I.1) can be rewritten as follows:

$$d_t = w_1 (r_t - r_t^*)^2 + w_2 (\Delta GS_t)^2 + w_3 (\Delta dr_t)^2 + w_4 (\Delta ar_t)^2 \quad \text{(I.1.a)}$$

where ΔGS_t = the change in the Reserve Banks' holdings of government securities in time t

Δdr_t = the change in the discount rate at the New York Reserve Bank in time t

Δar_t = the change in the buying rate on acceptance at the New York Reserve Bank in time t

w_i = the weight attached to each variable.

The other variables are defined as before. Formulation of the disutility function in this way does not, of course, exclude the possibility that the weight attached to any of the variables is zero.

It is assumed, then, that the Federal Reserve policy makers acted as though they were minimizing the disutility function (I.1.a) with respect to each of the policy variables (ΔGS_t, Δdr_t, and Δar_t) subject to the constraint imposed by their view of the workings of the credit market and the behavior of member banks in borrowing from the Reserve Banks. These constraints have been briefly discussed in the above section, and it is now necessary to give them explicit form.

The model of the money market assumed to be used by the Fed is as follows:

$$C_{d_t} = a_0 - a_1 r_t + a_2 O_t + a_3 SS_t \quad \text{(I.2)}$$

$$C_{S_t} = b_0 + b_1 r_t - b_2 B_t - b_3 B_{t-1} - b_4 dr_t - b_5 dr_{t-1} - b_6 ar_t - b_7 ar_{t-1}$$

where the new variables are defined as follows:

C_{d_t} = quantity of credit demanded in time t

Cs_t = quantity of credit supplied in time t

r_t = "the" short-term rate of interest in time t

O_t = output in time t

SS_t = speculation in the stock market in time t

B_t = member bank borrowings in time t

The demand equation incorporates the discussion of the previous section. It should be noted, however, that commodity speculation does not appear explicitly in the demand equation. The reason is that the output variable includes output for sale and output to be accumulated in inventories.

The supply equation embodies the Riefler-Burgess doctrine by making the supply of credit a negative function of member bank borrowings. Of course, member banks will not be willing to lend the same amount at the same rate if the cost of obtaining needed reserves increases. Hence, the discount and acceptance rates enter the supply function with negative signs.

The specific formulation of the supply equation in (I.2) assumes that the volume of indebtedness, the cost of indebtedness, and the cost of selling acceptances to the Fed all enter the supply equation on both a current and a lagged basis. These variables affect the willingness of member banks to lend both currently and with a one period lag due to the time necessary for the banks to adjust their portfolio positions.[16] Moreover, this formulation allows us to rewrite the supply equation, leaving the demand equation unchanged, to express the quantity of credit supplied as a function of the *changes* in borrowings, the discount rate, and the acceptance rate as follows:[17]

$$C_{d_t} = a_0 - a_1 r_t + a_2 O_t + a_3 SS_t \qquad \text{(I.2.a)}$$

$$C_{s_t} = b_0 + b_1 r_t - b_2 \Delta B_t - b'_3 B_{t-1}$$
$$- b_4 \Delta dr_t - b'_5 dr_{t-1} - b_6 \Delta ar_t - b'_7 ar_{t-1}$$

where the Δ's mean that first differences have been taken.

The supply equation in (I.2.a) is desirable because the open market policy of the Fed is expressed by purchases and sales of government securities (i.e., the change in its holdings of government securities). As will be shown, the change in member bank borrowing is a function of these purchases and sales. Likewise, for consistency, *changes* in the discount and acceptance rates are taken to be the correct expressions of these policy variables.

The system of equations (I.2.a) can be reduced to an expression for the short-term rate of interest as determined in the market for credit. Thus, setting $Cd_t = Cs_t$ of equations (I.2.a) yields

$$r_t = l_0 + l_1 O_t + l_2 SS_t + l_3 \Delta B_t + l_4 B_{t-1} + l_5 \Delta dr_t + l_6 dr_{t-1} + l_7 \Delta ar_t + l_8 ar_{t-1} \quad \text{(I.2.b)}$$

It remains only to specify the behavioral equation for the change in member-bank borrowing. This is done, in accordance with the reasoning of the previous section, in the following formulation:

$$\Delta B_t = c_0 + c_1 \Delta N_t - c_2 \Delta dr_{t-1} + c_3 \Delta ar_{t-1} \quad \text{(I.3)}$$

where ΔN_t = the change in "need" for reserves by member banks in time t (explained below).

The specification of this equation follows closely the argument presented in the previous section. The changes in the discount and acceptance rates have been lagged to allow for the time it takes for member banks to adjust their positions.[18] "Need" is not lagged, however, because the banks' reserve position must be adjusted immediately to need.

The problem that remains is to define precisely the "need" variable. The change in need is defined to be the change in required reserves less the change arising from all sources of reserves (other than borrowings) plus the change in uses of funds other than reserves. Or,

$$\Delta N_t \equiv \Delta RR_t - \Delta S_t^B + \Delta U_t^R \quad \text{(I.4)}$$

where ΔRR_t = changes in required reserves in time t.

ΔS_t^B = changes in sources of funds other than borrowings in time t (i.e., the sum of the changes in acceptances and government securities held by the Fed, other Reserve credit, the monetary gold stock, and treasury currency outstanding.)

ΔU_t^R = change in uses of funds other than reserves in time t (i.e., the sum of currency in circulation, Treasury cash holdings, and Treasury, nonmember, and other deposits with the Fed).

This definition of ΔN_t is, of course, based on the Reserve equation, and it is interesting to note that the change in "need" can also be defined, using the reserve equation, as[19]

$$\Delta N \equiv \Delta B_t - \Delta ER_t$$

where ΔER_t = changes in excess reserves in time t. In other words, ΔN_t is the negative of the change in free reserves.

If the change in excess reserves in time t is zero, the change in need is identical to the change in borrowing. It may well be that Fed officials had something more like this in mind than equation (I.3). These ideas are utilized later in the study and are brought up now only for the sake of completeness.

In order to demonstrate explicitly the dependence of the "need" variable on open market operations, the definition can be expanded as follows:

$$\Delta N_t \equiv \Delta RR_t - (\Delta S_t^{B.GS} + \Delta GS_t) + \Delta U_t^R$$
$$\equiv \Delta RR'_t - \Delta GS_t \qquad (I.4.a)$$

and

$$\Delta RR'_t \equiv \Delta RR_t - \Delta S_t^{B.GS} + \Delta U_t^R$$

where $\Delta S_t^{B.GS}$ = change in sources of funds other than borrowings and government securities.

ΔGS_t = change in the Fed's holdings of government securities (i.e., the open-market policy variable, purchases and sales of government securities).

Finally, it is necessary to define the "desired" level of the short-term rate. The desired level is defined as a function of the target variables the Fed would like to affect: output, speculation, and international financial stabilization. The desired level thus encompasses all possible goals, domestic and international.

It is apparent that the goal of international financial stabilization was virtually identical to Britain's returning to, and then remaining on, the gold standard.[20] This goal, in turn, depended on stopping and/or reversing the gold flow from Britain to the United States. As both Wicker and Clarke have pointed out, and as the minutes of the Open Market Investment Committee illustrate, Fed officials (Strong in particular) thought that the best way to do this would be to establish a "suitable" differential between short-term rates in New York and London. This was supposed to keep gold out of New York and attract it to London by keeping the rate earned in New York sufficiently below the rate earned in London.[21]

Therefore, the function defining the desired short-term rate of interest is

$$r_t^* = d_0 + d_1O_t + d_2SC_t + d_3SS_t + d_4r_{L_t} \qquad (I.5)$$

where O_t = output in time t

SC_t = commodity speculation in period t

SS_t = stock-market speculation in period t

r_{L_t} = the short-term interest rate in London.

The signs attached to the coefficients of the target variables in equation (I.5) are all clear with the possible exception of the sign on O_t. The reason for the positive sign on O_t is the assumption that the Fed was following a counter-cyclical policy. The tests to be done in the sequel will show whether or not this assumption is warranted. The signs on SC_t and SS_t are based upon the desire of Fed officials to stop speculation. Assuming speculation to be negatively related to the cost of obtaining funds to finance speculation, high interest rates are in order when speculation occurs. Finally, the sign on r_{L_t} is positive because of the desire to reverse the gold flow. If the short-term rate of interest in London falls (rises), the short-term rate in New York must also fall (can be permitted to rise).

The data to be used for each of the variables described in this section will be specified in a subsequent section. For now, it is sufficient to accept these variables in their abstract form.

The procedure now requires the substitution of equation (I.4.a) defining the need variable into equation (I.3) for the change in member bank borrowings. The results are then substituted for ΔBt in the reduced form equation (I.2.b) for r_t. Finally, the resulting equations for r_t and equation (I.5) for r_t* are substituted into the disutility function (I.1.a.). The minimization process then gives us the equation for open market purchases and sales of government securities, changes in the discount rate, and changes in the acceptance rate, that will insure minimum disutility for the policy makers. The process is straight forward but tedious and is therefore relegated to Appendix C. Only the resulting equations for the policy variables are reproduced here:

$$\begin{aligned} \Delta GS_t = &\pm A_0 - A_1O_t - A_2SS_t + A_3\ \Delta RR'_t - A_4SC_t \\ &- A_5r_{L_t} - A_6\ \Delta dr_{t-1} + A_7\ \Delta ar_{t-1} + A_8\ \Delta dr_t \\ &+ A_9\ \Delta ar_t + A_{10}B_{t-1}\ + A_{11}dr_{t-1} + A_{12}ar_{t-1} \end{aligned} \qquad (I.6)$$

$$\Delta dr_t = \pm B_0 + B_1 O_t + B_2 SS_t - B_3 \Delta N_t + B_4 SC_t + B_5 r_{L_t} + B_6 \Delta dr_{t-1} - B_7 \Delta ar_{t-1} - B_8 \Delta ar_t - B_9 B_{t-1} - B_{10} dr_{t-1} - B_{11} ar_{t-1} \quad (I.7)$$

$$\Delta ar_t = \pm C_0 + C_1 O_t + C_2 SS_t - C_3 \Delta N_t + C_4 SC_t + C_5 r_{L_t} + C_6 \Delta dr_{t-1} - C_7 \Delta ar_{t-1} - C_8 \Delta dr_t - C_9 B_{t-1} - C_{10} dr_{t-1} - C_{11} ar_{t-1} \quad (I.8)$$

The derivation of the signs of the coefficients in equations (I.6) - (I.8) is explained in Appendix C. It seems desirable, however, to discuss the meaning of the signs here. The discussion will center on the equation for open market purchases and sales, but applies to the equations for changes in the discount and acceptance rates as well. The only difference is that the coefficients on the variables in equations (I.7) and (I.8) have the opposite signs from those in equation (I.6) because an increase (decrease) in the discount or acceptance rate is restrictive (expansive) whereas a decrease (increase) in the purchases of government securities is restrictive (expansive).

The negative sign of the coefficient on output represents what is assumed to have been a countercyclical policy. To repeat, this assumption will be tested. The negative signs attached to the coefficients of the speculation variables indicate the desire to reduce speculation through tightening of the credit market. The negative sign on the coefficient for r_{L_t} indicates that rates in New York must be lowered (raised) if rates in London fall (rise) to prevent unwanted gold flows.

The positive sign on the coefficient of $\Delta RR'_t$ indicates that Fed officials took into account changes in sources and uses of reserve funds other than borrowings and government securities. The sign is positive because of the definition of $\Delta RR'_t$. Ceteris paribus, changes in other sources are offset by sales; changes in uses are offset by purchases; and changes in required reserves are offset by purchases. $\Delta RR'_t$ is then the variable that the Fed responds to in "defensive" operations—operations designed to "defend" member banks' reserves against exogenous changes.

The signs on the coefficients of Δdr_{t-1} and Δar_{t-1} reflect the assumption that the change in member bank borrowings in time t is a negative function of the change in the discount rate in period t-1 and a positive function of the change in the acceptance rate in period t-1. If all else is the same, but, for some unknown reason, the acceptance rate rises, member banks will borrow more. But this would lead to an undesired increase in interest rates. (Due to the assumption that all else is the same, any change in borrowing, and therefore the interest rate, is not desired.) The positive sign on the coefficient on Δar_{t-1} therefore indicates that this undesired change would be counteracted by increased purchases. Why would the acceptance rate rise if the other variables in equation (I.6) remained the same? This could possibly occur if the Fed changed the acceptance rate in response to factors not included in (I.7). It could be argued, for example, that the buying rate at the Fed was kept close to the open market rate on acceptances, but this latter rate is not included in (I.7). This point is discussed more fully later. A change in the discount rate, ceteris paribus, is harder to explain.

The remaining variables are best considered in groups. Both Δdr_t and Δar_t represent changes in policy variables concurrent with open market operations. Since an increase (the argument is symmetrical for a decrease) in the discount rate will serve, by itself, to increase the market rate (from equation [I.2.b.]) with the given volume of borrowing (by making that borrowing more costly), then the concurrent sales of government securities needed to force the banks into debt need not be as large (negatively) as if there were no increase in this rate. (Or, the concurrent purchases can be greater, if other changes call for purchases.) The argument for an increase in the acceptance rate is similar.[22]

Finally, B_{t-1}, dr_{t-1}, and ar_{t-1} reflect Fed policy in the past month, and, through the supply equation (I.2), the market for short-term credit in the present and in the past month. Policy this month therefore depends on policy and the state of the market (or at least the supply side of the market) *last* month. Assuming everything else to be the same, the tighter was the market *last* month, the less should sales be (or the more should purchases be) *this* month. This formulation reflects an attitude of waiting for the results of past changes before making further changes.

As previously stated, the coefficients in equations (I.7) and (I.8) are subject to the same interpretation as the coefficients of equations (I.6). The only point that needs discussion, therefore, is the coefficient of the variable ΔN_t which does not appear, per se, in (I.6).

If something happens to increase the need of member banks to borrow (for example, an outflow of gold or an increase in money in circulation) and if the increased borrowing by member banks due to this increased need is not to raise the market rate of interest, then it is necessary to counteract this increased need by lowering either the discount or acceptance rate, or both. Since $\Delta N_t \equiv \Delta RR'_t - \Delta GS_t$ (equation [I.4.a.]), it is obvious that purchases of government securities can be accompanied by a smaller increase (or a decrease) in the discount and acceptance rates than if there were no purchases. This is the complement of the coefficients of Δdr_t and Δar_t in equation (I.6) and is subject to the same interpretation. (The argument for sales is symmetrical.)

Before discussing the data used and reporting the results, the second model needs to be discussed. The results from the testing of both of these models will then be presented.

Model II: The Ultimate Target Variables as the Goals

The model developed in this section is more complex than Model I. The variables assumed to enter the disutility function in this case are the ultimate target variables of Federal Reserve policy. In a sense, this model is more complete since it takes the target variables explicitly into account, and therefore factors other than the interest rate that affect these target variables. But this increased completeness comes at the expense of greater complexity; and, in estimating, it is expensive in terms of degrees of freedom. There is also the criticism that the policy makers may very well *not* have had a model in mind more complete than the model of the short-term money market. This is part of the appeal of the first model. On the other hand, Model I may be criticized as incomplete for not taking many factors into account.

The disutility function in this model is assumed to be as follows:

$$d_t = w_1 (SS_t)^2 + w_2 (SC_t)^2 + w_3 (\Delta G_t - \Delta G_t^*)^2 - w_4 (O_{t+k})^2 + w_5 (\Delta GS_t)^2 + w_6 (\Delta dr_t)^2 + w_7 (\Delta ar_t)^2 \quad \text{(II.1)}$$

where d_t = the disutility in time t

SS_t = actual level of stock market speculation in time t

SC_t = actual level of commodity speculation in time t

ΔG_t = actual change in monetary gold stock in the United States in time t

ΔG_t^* = desired change in monetary gold stock of the United States in time t

O_{t+k} = actual output in some future time period

ΔGS_t, Δdr_t, and Δar_t are defined as before.

This formulation of the Fed's disutility function makes use of a point made earlier that it may be desirable to assume that the policy makers wanted to make some of the target variables as small or as large as possible. In (II.1) it is assumed that the Fed desires to make speculation in the stock market and in commodities as small as possible (preferably, zero). Hence, *any* commodity or stock market speculation adds to the disutility of the policy makers. On the other hand, the policy makers would like future output (the time need not be specified, as will become clear) to be as large as possible (perhaps at capacity). Therefore, the higher the level of output in the future, the lower the disutility of the Fed. The incorporation of O_{t+k} into the disutility function makes clear the policy dilemma facing the Fed in trying to stop speculation. This point is explored more fully below.

The disutility function (II.1) incorporates what are considered to be the most important goals of the policy makers based on the discussion in Chapter Two. The domestic goals are the promotion of production and distribution without encouraging speculation. Where speculation did occur, it is assumed that the Fed desired to stop it. The international goal was the restoration and maintenance of the international gold standard. This, in turn, was thought to depend upon stopping, and then reversing, the flow of gold into the United States. Hence, the disutility function is given the above form.

The model of the money market (through which the Fed influenced the economy) used in the present model is taken to be identical to the one developed in Model I with one exception. The current level of stock market speculation is taken below to be a function of two predetermined variables and the interest rate (see below, equation [II.5]). Therefore the current level of stock market speculation in the reduced-form equation for the short-term interest rate from Model I (equation [I.2.b]) is replaced by its predicted value based on these predetermined variables. This then gives us

$$r_t = l_0 + l_1 O_t + l_2 SS_{t-1} + l_3 S\dot{P}_t + l_4 \Delta B_t + l_5 B_{t-1} + l_6 \Delta dr_t + l_7 dr_{t-1} + l_8 \Delta ar_t + l_9 ar_{t-1} \quad \text{(II.2)}$$

The equation for changes in member bank borrowing (I.3) is taken directly from the first section:

$$\Delta B_t = c_0 + c_1 \Delta N_t - c_2 \Delta dr_{t-1} + c_3 \Delta ar_{t-1} \quad \text{(II.3)}$$

Finally, the definition of the "need" variable also remains the same. Using (I.4) and (I.4.a) gives us

$$\Delta N_t \equiv \Delta RR_t - \Delta S_t^B + \Delta U_t^R \quad \text{(II.4)}$$

and

$$\Delta N_t \equiv \Delta RR'_t - \Delta GS_t \quad \text{(II.4.a)}$$

where $\Delta RR'_t \equiv \Delta RR_t - \Delta S_t^{B.GS} + \Delta U^R_t$

The equations for SS_t, SC_t, ΔG_t, O_{t+k}, and the "desired" goldflow, G_t*, are specified below. A verbal explanation is then given.

$$SS_t = b_{10} + b_{11} SS_{t-1} - b_{12} r_t + b_{13} S\dot{P}_t \quad \text{(II.5)}$$

$$SC_t = b_{20} + b_{21} SC_{t-1} - b_{22} r_t + b_{23} P_t \quad \text{(II.6)}$$

$$\Delta G_t = b_{30} + b_{31} \Delta G_{t-1} + b_{32} (r_t - r_{L_t}) + b_{33} BT_t \quad \text{(II.7)}$$

$$\Delta G_t^* = a_{30} - a_{31} G_{t-1} + a_{32} ERS_t - a_{33} DG_t \quad \text{(II.8)}$$

$$O_{t+k} = b_{40} + b_{41} O_t - b_{42} r_t + b_{43} \dot{P}_t \quad \text{(II.9)}$$

where the variables not previously defined are defined as follows:

$S\dot{P}_t$ = the current expected rate of increase in stock prices

$\dot{P}_t$ = the current expected rate of increase in commodity prices

BT_t = the balance of trade for the United States in period t

G_{t-1} = the monetary stock of gold in the United States in period t-1

ERS_t = the exchange rate for sterling in dollars per pound in time t

DG_t = a dummy variable valued at one prior to Britain's return to gold in April, 1925, and at zero thereafter (i.e., a dummy variable representing the desire for a return to the gold standard).

Each of the equations defining the actual values of the target variables bears one point in common—the dependent variable in each case is a function of a lagged value of that variable. Wood defended this approach on the grounds that not all of the predetermined variables influencing the dependent (or jointly determined) variables are known,

> . . . but, whatever they are, they have been causing [the dependent variable] . . . to, say, rise in recent periods. Hence, given the [known predetermined variables] . . . our best guess is that the unspecified predetermined variables will continue to exert an upward influence on [the dependent variable] . . . during the current period.[23]

In other words, Wood used lagged values of the dependent variables in place of all of the unknown variables left out of the equation in order to minimize the specification error involved in omitting some of the predetermined variables. It is conceivable that Federal Reserve officials may well have been dependent on past values in their forecast of present values. The explanation of the equations that follows considers the propriety of including lagged values in each separate case.

Equation (II.5) expresses the dependence of stock market speculation in this time period on the current cost of borrowed funds, the current increase of stock prices (or the expected increase), and the extent of speculation in the previous period. In this case it is probably appropriate to express the existence and extent of speculation now on previous speculation. The speculative fever in the late 1920's undoubtedly fed upon itself and was a cumulative movement. Stock market speculation was undoubtedly believed by Fed officials to be a negative function of the rate of interest. They apparently sought in 1928 and 1929 to bring speculation on the stock market to an end by making credit more costly and more difficult to obtain. Finally, stock market speculation is a positive function of the expected increase in stock prices since it is the hope of the speculator to make capital gains. (The exact definition of $\dot{SP}_t$, as for all the variables, is left to the next section.)

The specification of the equation for speculation in commodities (II.6) is similar to that for speculation on the stock market. An expected increase in prices encourages building up inventories in expectation of the higher prices. An increase in the cost and difficulty of obtaining funds to finance the carrying of these inventories will discourage the speculative buildup, hence the negative coefficient on the short-term interest rate. Finally, commodity speculation may also be taken to be cumulative in its effect, although the case is not as strong here as with the stock market.

It is assumed in equation (II.7) that the Fed believed gold flows to be positively related to the New York-London interest rate differential and to the U.S. balance of trade. Gold flows are also taken to be cumulative, and therefore the lagged value is again included.

The gold flow *desired* by Federal Reserve officials (II.8) is a negative function of the U.S. monetary gold stock. In the early part of the period, the Fed thought that the U.S. had more than "its share" of the world's gold and that it was essential that some of this be lost to Europe to strengthen their currency if the gold standard was to be restored and maintained. Later, after Britain left the gold standard in September, 1931, the excuse given for raising the discount and acceptance rates was the reduction of the U.S. gold stock. Therefore, the desired flow of gold appears to have been a negative function of the stock of monetary gold held by the United States.

Since the restoration and maintenance of the gold standard appears to have been equivalent to " . . . the restoration of sterling to its pre-war parity . . . "[24] it seems reasonable to assume that the desired gold flow was a positive function of the exchange rate for sterling, or at least, of the difference between the existing rate and the parity rate.[25] The lower the exchange rate, the more essential it was that Britain receive a larger inflow of gold to strengthen that rate (or that the U.S. experience an outflow or a smaller inflow). Later, in 1927, when the exchange rate slipped toward the bottom of its range consistent with keeping sterling on gold, it was thought desirable once again to reduce the inflow of gold to the U.S. or induce an outflow.[26]

It is further assumed that an outflow of gold was desired prior to Britain's return to gold. Therefore the dummy variable for the period prior to Britain's return is expected to have a negative coefficient.

Finally, equation (II.9) expresses the apparent belief by Fed officials, discussed and documented in Chapter Two, that current high interest rates can negatively affect output six to twelve months in the future.[27] They appear also to have believed that general price increases (or expected price increases) would stimulate a response on the supply side and encourage greater output, provided that the economy was not operating at capacity.[28] The present level of output is also included in equation (II.9) since the level of output in the immediate future is undoubtedly a positive function of output today (output is highly autocorrelated for short lags). The goal of maximizing output in the near future is not greatly different from maximizing output in the present.

The set of equations (II.5) - (II.9) illustrates many of the points made earlier (in Chapter Two). The model appears to be consistent with what Fed officials were saying. Monetary policy should be tight when there was danger of speculation, yet this policy should be tempered by the desire to achieve maximum output. And, it was desirable during most of the period that the United States lose gold. Nevertheless, it was the loss of gold in late 1931 that was identified by the officials as the reason for tightening credit. Increasing prices may call forth increasing output if the economy is not operating at capacity, but they may also induce commodity speculation. And so forth.

The procedure followed in deriving the equations for open market purchases and sales and changes in the discount and acceptance rates is the same as before. It involves substituting equation (II.4a) into equation (II.3) and the result into equation (II.2) thus linking the interest rate with open-market operations. The resulting equation for r_t is then substituted into equations (II.5) - (II.9) and the results are used in the disutility function (II.1). Taking the appropriate partial derivatives, setting them equal to zero, and solving for the policy variables yields the desired equations. As before, the process is contained in Appendix C with only the result included here.

$$\Delta GS_t = \pm A_0 - A_1 SS_{t-1} - A_2 S\dot{P}_t - A_3 O_t$$
$$- A_4 SC_{t-1} - A_5 \dot{P}_t - A_6 rL_t + A_7 BT_t + A_8 \Delta G_{t-1}$$
$$+ A_9 G_{t-1} - A_{10} ERS_t + A_{11} DG_t + A_{12} \Delta RR'_t$$

$$- A_{13}\Delta dr_{t-1} + A_{14}\Delta ar_{t-1} + A_{15}\Delta dr_t + A_{16}\Delta ar_t$$
$$+ A_{17}B_{t-1} + A_{18}dr_{t-1} + A_{19}ar_{t-1} \qquad \text{(II.10)}$$

$$\Delta dr_t = \pm B_0 + B_1SS_{t-1} + B_2S\dot{P}_t + B_3O_t$$
$$+ B_4SC_{t-1} + B_5\dot{P}_t + B_6rL_t - B_7BT_t - B_8\Delta G_{t-1}$$
$$- B_9G_{t-1} + B_{10}ERS_t - B_{11}DG_t - B_{12}\Delta N_t + B_{13}\Delta dr_{t-1}$$
$$- B_{14}\Delta ar_{t-1} - B_{15}\Delta ar_t - B_{16}B_{t-1} - B_{17}dr_{t-1} - B_{18}ar_{t-1} \qquad \text{(II.11)}$$

$$\Delta ar_t = \pm C_0 + C_1SS_{t-1} + C_2S\dot{P}_t + C_3O_t$$
$$+ C_4SC_{t-1} + C_5\dot{P}_t + C_6rL_t - C_7BT_t - C_8\Delta G_{t-1}$$
$$- C_9G_{t-1} + C_{10}ERS_t - C_{11}DG_t - C_{12}\Delta N_t$$
$$+ C_{13}\Delta dr_{t-1} - C_{14}\Delta ar_{t-1} - C_{15}\Delta dr_t - C_{16}B_{t-1}$$
$$- C_{17}dr_{t-1} - C_{18}ar_{t-1} \qquad \text{(II.12)}$$

Many of the same comments made regarding Model I are applicable here as well. These will not be repeated, but it may be instructive to consider the differences between equations (II.10) - (II.12) and the corresponding equations from Model I (equations [I.6] - [I.8]).

The obvious difference is in the number of variables involved, which is the result of the more complete specification given in Model II. Each of the target variables appearing in equations (I.6) - (I.8) is replaced in equations (II.10) - (II.12) by the predetermined variables in the equations that are assumed to illustrate the model of the economy that the Fed thought was applicable.

In addition, the predetermined variables in the assumed structural equation for current gold flows appear in the second model along with the variables assumed to determine the "desired" gold flow.

Each of the variables has the sign that would be expected if the Fed were attempting to (1) follow a counter cyclical policy (i.e., stabilize the economy), (2) prevent or stop speculation, and (3) promote the return and maintenance of the international gold standard.

The Time Period and the Data Used in Testing

The above models were tested using monthly data for the years 1924-1931 inclusive, although this excludes the year 1923. The reason for this exclusion is the lack of data needed in the construction of the open market policy variable (ΔGS') prior to December, 1923. This is more fully explained below.

It is not considered desirable to begin the test period before 1923 because prior to that year open market operations were not coordinated for the purpose of implementing a System policy. Although an informal committee of governors was established in 1922, it was not until the establishment of the Open Market Investment Committee (in April, 1923) that a single body was responsible for the coordination of open market purchases and sales.[29] It was not until the end of 1923 that a System Account was established.

The test period was not extended past the end of 1931 because of the numerous additional factors that evolved in the beginning of 1932. The passage of the Glass-Stegal Act in February of that year permitted the use of government securities as collateral for outstanding Federal Reserve Notes. Soon thereafter the Fed began buying government securities, ostensibly because the new act enabled them to do so. Prior to the passage of the Act, the Fed did not have enough eligible paper to provide collateral and was therefore making up the difference by pledging gold. The passage of the Glass-Stegal Act, by permitting government securities to be offered as collateral for Federal Reserve notes, increased the Fed's free gold by almost one billion dollars. The Fed was then able to pursue an easier money policy without concern for the loss of gold that such a policy might entail.[30]

Friedman and Schwartz reject this explanation on the grounds that the amount of free gold could have increased in other ways even prior to the passage of the Glass-Stegal Act. By their interpretation, the substantial purchases in early 1932 were the result of Congressional pressure on the Fed to *do* something or else face new legislation forcing them to act.[31] Either way, the year 1932 contained extraordinary factors not present in earlier years.[32]

In addition, it was during 1932 that member banks began to pile up a large volume of excess reserves. This, of course, was counter to prevailing System opinion about the behavior of the banks and makes questionable the models assumed to have been operating prior to that year.[33]

For these reasons, the time period used in the tests of the hypotheses is restricted to the years 1923 through 1931. This should be sufficient to answer the question of why the Fed failed to respond to the contraction that began in late 1929, whether the answer lay in the goals or inconsistent behavior.

The data used are reported fully in Appendix A. It seems advisable, however, to point out some of the problems encountered with the availability and reliability of the data used before reporting the results of the tests.

The two most difficult problems encountered were (1) the lack of data on required or excess reserves and (2) the choice of an indicator of stock market speculation.

There are no monthly data on excess reserves (or required reserves) available prior to 1929. These data are, however, available for call dates. A method for estimating required reserves was developed and these estimates were used for the years prior to 1929. Beginning in 1929, the available data were employed. The estimation method is described at length in Appendix A. It should be sufficient here simply to briefly describe the estimating technique.

Regression analysis was employed to estimate the effective required reserve ratio as a function of the ratio of net demand to time deposits and a time trend for call-date data. The results were surprisingly good.

Based on the estimated relationship, monthly data for member banks on demand and time deposits were then used to estimate the effective reserve ratio monthly. This was then applied to total member bank deposits to estimate required reserves.

There is no satisfactory method available for determining the reliability of the estimated data thus obtained. There is, however, a means of determining whether or not its use in the regression analysis might lead to erroneous conclusions.

During the years 1923-1928, there was apparently little concern about excess reserves. This was evidently the result of their low level. If it can be assumed that excess reserves were not only low but fairly stable, then this would seem to justify ignoring their existence.[34] This being the case, the change in all sources, other than borrowings and purchases and sales of government securities, plus the change in all uses, other than reserves, could be used as the variable entering equations (I.6) and (II.9) to represent "defensive" operations. A similar argument holds for the change-in-need variable in the equations for changes in the discount and acceptance rates.[35]

As a check against erroneous conclusions based on poor estimates of the "defensive" variable $\Delta RR'_t$, the regressions were also run using the variable described in the preceding paragraph in place of $\Delta RR'_t$. The results of these tests do not differ from the results when $\Delta RR'_t$ was used.

The second major problem was the choice of an indicator of stock market speculation. Throughout the minutes of the meetings of the Open Market Investment Committee there are numerous references to brokers' loans.[36] However, a statement by Strong provides a key to what was perhaps considered by the policy makers to be a better indicator—the differential between bond and stock yields.[37] This differential should, indeed, reflect any speculative activity in the market.

If the yield on stocks declines relative to the yield on bonds while the volume of stocks increases, this indicates a shift in the preferences of creditors away from bonds to stocks.[38] This could of course, be due to any one of a number of factors, only one of which is speculation. But the drastic change in the relationship of the yields in the 1927-1929 period is consistent with an interpretation that places the primary responsibility for this shift on speculation in the stock market.[39] (See Table A.I, Appendix A.)

There is no completely acceptable indicator of stock market speculation, but the differential between bond and stock yields is believed to be a good, although imperfect, indicator. For this reason, it was used in the tests reported below, but in a modified form.

The variable actually used in the results reported below, XSS, is the product of the variable described above (SS) and a dummy variable taken to be equal to one in the months from November, 1927, through September, 1930, and zero in all other months. In other words, the variable used in the regression results reported below has a value of zero for all months except November, 1927, through September, 1930, when it is equal to the difference between bond and stock yields. There were several reasons for this change, and it might be justifiable on several counts.

The Fed did not appear to be concerned with stock market speculation prior to the last months of 1927. This was noted in Chapter

Two where it was seen that the Fed pursued its easy money policy of 1927 with full knowledge that such a course might stimulate the stock market. It was also noted there that the Fed's attention seemed to turn *completely* to the stock market in early 1928 through the panic in late 1929. The variable was allowed to maintain a non-zero value into 1930, however, to test the hypothesis that it was, at least in part, the fear of further stimulation of the stock market that restrained Federal Reserve officials from pursuing an easier money policy in the first half of the year. Furthermore, as was reported in Chapter Two, it was not until June, 1930, that Harrison expressed the belief that the System need not fear any further speculation in the stock market.

As a result of these considerations, the indicator of stock market speculation was taken to be equal to the difference between yield on bonds and the yield on stocks in November, 1927, when this difference rose above zero, and ending in October, 1930, when it again fell below zero.

It should be noted that this treatment of the indicator of stock market speculation might imply either the absence of speculation in any period other than November, 1927, through September, 1930, or the absence of any desire to control stock market speculation as a goal of the System except in that period.

While the problems described above were the most difficult, they were not the only problems encountered. A problem similar to that of an appropriate indicator of stock market speculation was encountered for commodity speculation. There was not an abundance of information available at the time on inventories, but there were several alternatives.[40] Several of these were tried, but none proved to be significant, and most had the wrong sign.[41]

It was decided, on the basis of the preliminary tests, that either there was no satisfactory indicator or there was no commodity speculation in this period. The latter conclusion was accepted because of the lack of expression of concern by Federal Reserve officials. At no time did they indicate a belief that commodity speculation was actually taking place, and no reference to indicators of commodity speculation were found during the investigation. This is in marked contrast to the open concern and comment on stock market speculation later in the period.

As a result of the above conclusions, it was decided that the most appropriate approach was to omit the SC variable and it does not enter the results reported below. This does not mean that the prevention of commodity speculation was not a goal; it means only that it did not appear at any time during the period under examination.[42]

The only other problem of any consequence was in finding appropriate variables to represent the "expected" rate of increase in wholesale prices and stock market prices. The variables $\dot{P}$ and $S\dot{P}$ were constructed using a weighted average of the rate of increase in prices (wholesale or stock market price indices) over the past three months. The weights used were geometrically declining weights.[43] Again, these are not totally satisfactory constructions; but they seem to be useful approximations.

Finally, the variable representing open market purchases and sales must be defined. There were several possibilities. One of these was the sum of the changes in the Fed's holdings of government securities *and* acceptances.[44] For reasons previously explained, it was deemed desirable, however, to exclude acceptances and explain changes in the acceptance rate as one of the policy variables of the Fed. (See Chapter Two.)

Given that the policy variable was to be changes in the holdings of government securities only, there still remained several alternatives. Data are available, beginning December, 1923, for four classifications of government securities held by the Federal Reserve System: (1) securities held in the System Account, (2) holdings of one- and two-day Treasury certificates, (3) holdings of government securities under resale agreement, and (4) other holdings in individual Reserve Bank accounts. The variable used in the regressions reported below ($\Delta GS'_t$) is the change in the sum of (1) and (4) *net* of changes associated with quarterly tax operations by the Treasury, for reasons explained below.

For several days around the fifteenth of March, June, September, and December, the Federal Reserve System engaged in two operations that had opposite effects. On the one hand, they purchased one- or two-day Treasury Certificates to provide the Treasury with operating funds during these quarterly tax-collection periods.[45] On the other hand, they sold securities from the System Account for these few days in order to absorb excess funds in the market as a result of Treasury redemptions around the same time and the increased float.[46]

The volume of the purchases of one- and two-day Treasury Certificates was greater than the open-market sales. This is supported in the results reported below, but can be seen by a casual inspection of the data. The effects of these operations were removed from ΔGS' by (1) not including holdings of one- or two-day Treasury certificates and (2) taking the average holdings in the System Account and in individual Reserve Bank accounts on days *other than* the days during which the Treasury operations took place. That the removal of this factor was successful is evidenced by the spectral analysis in Appendix B (Chart B. III).

Finally, purchases of securities under resale agreement were excluded from ΔGS' because the initiative in these purchases did not rest with the Fed. Rather, the initiative came from dealers in government securities.

In order to insure a market for government securities, the Fed stood ready to buy government securities from dealers in any amount at a stated rate. Hence, the control over the volume of these securities bought was an indirect control—a control through rate only. The securities thus obtained were sold back to the dealers within fifteen days.[47] Burgess states that ". . . the transaction in which Federal Reserve open-market policy finds its most important expression is the outright purchase or sale of United States Government obligations."[48]

It is the exclusion of purchases made under resale agreements that prohibits the construction of ΔGS' for any month prior to December, 1923. Data on average daily holdings of government securities under repurchase agreement could not be found or constructed and could therefore not be taken out of ΔGS.

Actually, it would do little harm to allow the Treasury-related operations to remain and make allowance for their existence by inserting dummy variables in equations (I.6) and (II.10) above for March, June, September, and December. In fact, as a check on the results obtained below, this was done. The results (some of which are reported below) support the results using ΔGS'. The effects of these operations were removed to simplify the analysis and focus on the primary questions involved in this thesis.[49]

Use of $\Delta GS'$ meant starting the regressions in 1924 instead of 1923, as previously noted. However, since the estimates of required reserves could not be obtained before April, 1923, starting in January, 1924, entails the loss of only eight months (because of first differencing). Furthermore, the loss of degrees of freedom is only four since use of the change in total holdings of government securities (ΔGS) requires using four additional variables (dummy variables for March, June, September, and December).

A list of the data, along with further explanations, is contained in Appendix A. The results of the tests using these data are reported below, first for Model I and then for Model II.[50]

Results of Tests of Model I

Equations (I.6) - (I.8) of Model I were fit to the data described in the preceding section and/or in Appendix A. The resulting regression equations are summarized in Table I. In this table, the coefficient of each independent variable is listed with the associated sample "t" statistic in parentheses below. The coefficient of determination. adjusted for degrees of freedom ($\bar{R}^2$), and the Durbin-Watson statistic (D.W.) are given beside each equation.

Table I actually contains three different equations for purchases and sales of government securities and for changes in the acceptance rate, and four different equations for changes in the discount rate. Equations (I.6.a), (I.7.a), and (I.8.a) are the regression results for equations (I.6) - (I.8). The others are alternative formulations that make use of the interrelationships of some of the independent variables in these three equations.

In the discussion of the final results developed in Model I, it was noted that certain groups of variables have a common element. It was there discussed that B_{t-1}, dr_{t-1}, and ar_{t-1} are a reflection of Federal Reserve policy in the previous period and therefore the supply side of the credit market in both the present and the previous period (from equations [I.2]). Hence, these three variables could justifiably be combined into *one* variable to represent the state of the supply side of the credit market prior to Federal Reserve policy changes.

TABLE I
REGRESSION RESULTS FOR MODEL I

Inter.	O_t	XSS_t	$\Delta RR'_t$ or ΔN_t	$r_{L,t}$	Δdr_{t-1}	Δar_{t-1}	Δdr_t	Δar_t	B_{t-1}	dr_{t-1}	ar_{t-1}	$\bar{R}^2$ DW	Equation Number
Open market operations:													
135.3 (2.76)	-2.38 (-4.18)	-11.61 (-1.22)	.030 (.84)	7.63 (1.49)	-13.57 (-.93)	-40.12 (-2.40)	-39.59 (-2.40)	.173 (.01)	.033 (1.20)	20.20 (1.40)	-1.86 (-.12)	.49 1.73	(I.6.a)
							($IDRP_t$		) (	IMC_{t-1}	)		
235.7 (4.51)	-2.47 (-5.39)	-13.49 (-1.48)	.037 (1.09)	7.02 (1.46)	-14.62 (-1.00)	-36.92 (-2.24)	-9.59 (-3.85)			15.76 (3.83)		.48 1.76	(I.6.b)
							($IDRP_t$		) (	r_{t-1}	)		
118.6 (3.44)	-2.44 (-5.23)	-13.24 (-1.44)	.040 (1.17)	8.29 (1.75)	-13.48 (-.92)	-32.12 (-1.92)	-8.83 (-3.36)			25.54 (3.61)		.47 1.79	(I.6.c)
Changes in the discount rate:													
.812 (2.59)	-.0064 (-1.73)	.0300 (.47)	-.00004 (-.16)	-.0202 (-.59)	-.3040 (-.35)	-.0660 (-.58)	—	.8991 (10.28)	.0002 (.85)	-.4107 (-4.75)	.4024 (4.08)	.69 2.16	(I.7.a)
									(	IMC_{t-1}	)		
-.034 (-.09)	-.0009 (-.25)	.0829 (1.23)	-.00002 (-.07)	.0244 (.69)	-.0340 (-.31)	-.0611 (-.49)	—	.8737 (10.10)		-.0111 (-.36)		.62 1.96	(I.7.b)

TABLE I *(Continued)*

Inter.	O_t	XSS_t	$\Delta RR'_t$ or ΔN_t	r_L	Δdr_{t-1}	Δar_{t-1}	Δdr_t	Δar_t	B_{t-1}	dr_{t-1}	ar_{t-1}		$\bar{R}^2$ DW	Equation Number
-.092 (-.24)	-.0006 (-.17)	.1529 (2.05)	.00005 (.20)	.0300 (.85)	-.1113 (-.98)	.0261 (.20)	—	.8656 (10.18)	(	IMC_{t-1} -.0150 (-.49)	)	XDA_t -.2560 (-2.04)	.63 1.96	(I.7.c)
.031 (.12)	-.0009 (-.26)	.1478 (1.99)	.00005 (.21)	.0262 (.76)	-.1111 (-.97)	.0228 (.18)	—	.8681 (9.72)	(	r_{t-1} -.0168 (-.32)	)	XDA_t -.2531 (-2.02)	.63 1.96	(I.7.d)
Changes in the acceptance rate:														
-.974 (-3.91)	.0103 (3.54)	.0048 (.09)	.00028 (1.48)	.0799 (2.96)	.0892 (.95)	-.0541 (-.66)	.6231 (10.28)	—	.0002 (.99)	.2383 (3.10)	-.4092 (-5.25)		.74 2.07	(I.8.a)
-.597 (-1.85)	.0033 (1.16)	.0102 (.18)	.00022 (1.03)	.0618 (2.11)	-.0706 (-.77)	.1451 (1.40)	.6210 (10.10)	—	(	IMC_{t-1} -.0564 (-2.20)	)		.67 1.94	(I.8.b)
-.235 (-1.14)	.0047 (1.70)	.0298 (.53)	.00018 (.85)	.0673 (2.44)	-.0747 (-.84)	.1130 (1.10)	.5929 (9.61)	—	(	r_{t-1} -.1270 (-3.02)	)		.68 1.91	(I.8.c)

Notes: Figures in parentheses below the reported coefficients are the associated sample t statistics. As indicated in the text, some of the independent variables are combined by principal component analysis into one variable. this is the case for IDRP and IMC. Finally, the coefficient of determination ($\bar{R}^2$) has been adjusted for degrees of freedom.

There is an additional reason for choosing to combine these variables: all three are highly correlated. Malinvaud suggests combining variables that exhibit a high degree of collinearity through the use of principal component analysis. Using the first principal component to replace the collinear variables reduces the number of independent variables and does not greatly affect the predictive ability of the regression equation if the first principal component accounts for most of the common variation in the original variables.[51]

The variables B_{t-1}, dr_{t-1}, and ar_{t-1}, have been replaced by their first principal component, designated IMC_{t-1}, in equations (I.6.b), (I.7.b), (I.7.c), and (I.8.b), in Table I. In a similar manner, Δdr_t and Δar_t have been replaced by their first principal component, designated $IDRP_t$, in equations (I.6.b) and (I.6.c).[52] These new variables may be thought of as an indicator of the condition of the supply side of the credit market prior to this month's Federal Reserve operations, and an indicator of the current changes in the Fed's rate policy, respectively.

Since IMC_{t-1} is the linear combination of the predetermined variables affecting the supply side of the market for credit, it is reasonable to assume that it should be closely correlated with the short-term rate of interest. This is, in fact, true. The simple correlation coefficient between IMC and r is .98. In equations (I.6.c), (I.7.d), and (I.8.c), r_{t-1} is substituted for IMC_{t-1} on the grounds that the two contain basically the same information from both a statistical and an economic point of view.

The formulations (I.6.c), (I.7.d), and (I.8.c) can be justified independently of the reasoning described above. Federal Reserve policy in this period is a function of the state of the credit market, which it is acting to influence, before it acts. The tighter (easier) credit is last month, the less it is necessary to tighten (ease) credit this month, ceteris paribus. This is, interestingly, precisely what Brunner and Meltzer believe to have happened—the Fed looked at the interest rate as *the* indicator of the state of the credit market before it acted.

It should be apparent from this digression that equations (I.6.c), (I.7.d), and (I.8.c) are equivalent in all important respects to the initial formulations (I.6.a), (I.7.a) and (I.8.a). The discussion of the results below centers around the former group of equations, but the discussion is also applicable to the latter group.

Before proceeding to the results, however, one further digression is necessary. It is essential to make clear the criterion for accepting or rejecting a hypothesis applied to the regression coefficients in Table I (and in subsequent tables as well).

Since the equations of Model I are specified with the expected signs on each of the coefficients, and since these signs are an integral part of the hypotheses to be tested, the appropriate test is a one-tailed test. If alpha is taken to be .10, the critical value of t for the coefficients in Table I is 1.29 if the hypothesized relationship is positive, -1.29 if it is negative.[53] These are the critical values used in the discussion below to determine whether or not the hypothesis is supported by the results. In cases where the hypothesis is not supported because the coefficient has the wrong sign, but the t statistic is large (absolutely), an attempt is made to explain why this result was obtained. The hypothesis tests are all made recognizing the well-known problems inherent in using such tests with time series data. The results should be interpreted with these problems in mind.

It may be seen from Table I that the coefficients of output (O_t), stock market speculation (XSS_t), and the level of interest rates in the previous month (r_{t-1}) in equation (I.6.c) for open market operations meet the criterion established above. Therefore the null hypothesis can be rejected in each of these cases in favor of the alternative hypotheses implicit in the signs attached to these coefficients in the development of Model I.

Based on these results it can be concluded that open market purchases and sales were intended to be countercyclical, but that monetary policy in 1928-1929 was designed to stop stock market speculation, and that the rise in XSS_t from early- to mid-1930 was partially responsible for the hesitancy of the open-market committee to purchase large amounts of government securities at that time. It would appear also from these results that Fed officials *did* use the prevailing short-term interest rate as a guide to policy. In particular, the low interest rates in 1930 and early 1931 were also partially responsible for the failure of the Fed to undertake large purchases. The Brunner-Meltzer hypothesis appears to be at least partly verified.

None of the other t statistics permit the rejection of the corresponding null hypothesis. In particular, the sign of the coefficient of r_{L_t} is positive instead of negative. The development of Model I suggested that this sign should be negative so that a decline in short-term rates in London would require greater purchases by the Fed to drive down rates in New York, ceteris paribus. The positive sign on r_{L_t} in equation (I.6.c) indicates just the opposite policy—a decline in rates in London would be met with fewer purchases or more sales of securities by the Fed which would *raise* interest rates in New York, ceteris paribus. This would obviously work *against* stopping a gold inflow.

The failure of the coefficient of $\Delta RR'_t$ to confirm the defensive nature of Federal Reserve open market operations is somewhat surprising. This is true also of the results for Model II reported below. A possible reason for obtaining this strange result is offered in the conclusion to this chapter.

The "wrong" sign of the coefficient of $IDRP_t$ is not nearly as surprising. This result could easily have been predicted. The reason for the negative coefficient is undoubtedly the use of changes in the discount and acceptance rates (especially the former) in unison with open market operations; that is, increases (decreases) in the discount and acceptance rates were used as supplements to sales (purchases) of government securities. Federal Reserve officials possibly viewed changes in rates as complements to open market operations, not as substitutes as implied in this model.[54] The negative signs on Δdr_{t-1} and Δar_{t-1} are probably a reflection of the complementary nature of rate changes and open market operations. This effect overrides any consideration of the effects of these rates on borrowings. This, it may be recalled, was the reason for the predicted signs on Δdr_{t-1} (negative) and Δar_{t-1} (positive) in the development of Model I.

With regard to changes in policy rates, an examination of equations (I.7.d) and (I.8.c) leads to the conclusion that changes in the discount rate (but not the acceptance rate) were used in the 1928-1930 period to combat stock market speculation while changes in the acceptance rate (but not the discount rate) were counter cyclical *and* designed to keep short-term rates in New York in the proper relation with their counterpart in London (or at least were used to move rates in New York in the same direction as rates in London).

The above conclusions must be tempered, however, by the considerable dependence of current changes in both of these rates on the simultaneous change in the other rate. This positive dependence is counter to the predicted negative relationship between changes in each of the rates. This is probably the result of a desire by Federal Reserve officials to keep the discount and acceptance rates in line both with each other and with market rates in general.[55] Again, this consideration, and the use of changes in the rates as complements rather than as substitutes, outweigh the substitutability of Δdr and Δar implicit in the development of Model I.

Equations (I.7.c) and (I.7.d) for changes in the discount rate contain a variable not previously defined. This variable, XDA, is a dummy variable representing the use of "direct action" as a policy substitute for raising the discount rate from February through June or July, 1929. The variable is given a value of one during this period and zero at other times.[56] The coefficient of this variable should be negative since the use of direct action (or direct pressure) was, indeed, a substitute for raising the discount rate. (This problem and the conflict between the New York Reserve Bank and the Federal Reserve Board were discussed in Chapter Two.) Had the policy of direct pressure not been adopted, it is likely that there would have been an increase in the discount rate to try to stop stock market speculation.

The coefficient of XDA_t in equation (I.7.d) does, in fact, have a negative sign. According to this estimate, the discount rate should (or would) have been raised 1/4 of one percent in each of the months during which direct action was substituted for changing the discount rate. Since the period of direct action lasted five months, this would indicate a total increase of 1 1/4 percent. In August, when the rate was finally raised, it was raised by one percent.

The dummy variable XDA_t and the variable XSS_t are the only variables in equation (I.7.d) that support the hypotheses of Model I. As previously noted, the coefficient of Δar_t is probably a reflection of the complementary nature of changes in the discount and acceptance rates.

None of the other hypotheses regarding changes in the discount rate are supported. The results are not favorable to the conclusion that discount rate changes were undertaken for either countercyclical or international reasons. Nor do changes in the discount rate appear to have been influenced by the prior state of the market.[57]

Exactly the opposite conclusions seem to hold for changes in the acceptance rate (equation [I.8.c]). While changes in the acceptance rate were apparently *not* influenced by stock market speculation, they apparently *were* designed to be counter-cyclical and favorable to the international goal of restoration of the gold standard. It would appear, too, that changes in the acceptance rate were negatively dependent on the prior state of the market as the development of Model I suggested.

In an effort to determine whether the conclusions regarding open market operations would be changed by the division of the period into sub-periods of particular interest, and at the same time to provide evidence on the Friedman-Schwartz hypothesis of inconsistent behavior, the period was divided at two different points—January, 1928 and January, 1929. The results of regressions run on these different sub-periods (1924-1927, 1928-1931 and 1924-1928, 1929-1931) are reported in Table II. The results of regressions starting in 1924 but ending at different points in time (December, 1929; December, 1930, and June, 1931) are also reported in Table II.[58]

As previously described, Friedman and Schwartz's explanation of the failure of the Federal Reserve to purchase large amounts of securities after 1929 is based on the inconsistency of its behavior before and after 1929.[59] Since they do not provide a definite point of division, the two divisions above were chosen because, while Benjamin Strong died in October, 1928, he was absent frequently during 1928 because of illness or visits abroad. Hence, it could be argued that his influence actually began to wane before his death.[60]

Finally, the division of the period into the sub-periods 1924-1927 and 1928-1931 should provide some indication of whether or not the international goals were more important before 1928 than after. This, it should be recalled, is the implication of Clarke's study.[61]

TABLE II
SUB-PERIOD ANALYSIS OF OPEN MARKET OPERATIONS (MODEL I)

Inter.	0_t	XSS_t	$\Delta RR'_t$	r_{L_t}	r_{t-1}	Δdr_{t-1}	Δar_{t-1}	$IDRP_t$	$\bar{R}^2$ DW
1924-1927:									
78.7	-2.74	—	.0290	16.67	34.68	-46.20	-12.51	-8.21	.45
(.91)	(-2.11)		(.66)	(1.14)	(2.75)	(-1.58)	(-.40)	(-1.40)	2.14
1928-1931:									
158.4	-2.89	-3.15	.0597	4.43	29.10	-5.80	-37.35	-8.40	.45
(2.50)	(-3.31)	(-.20)	(1.12)	(.64)	(2.48)	(-.30)	(-1.63)	(-2.56)	1.47
1924-1928:									
79.5	-3.23	-31.35	.0308	23.61	39.44	-30.18	-17.17	-11.03	.47
(.92)	(-2.62)	(-1.43)	(.73)	(1.67)	(3.30)	(-1.15)	(-.58)	(-2.08)	1.94
1929-1931:									
-166.2	1.42	-77.66	.0802	13.41	6.09	8.39	-40.08	-4.67	.59
(-1.99)	(1.27)	(-3.83)	(1.65)	(2.08)	(.55)	(.51)	(-2.15)	(-1.62)	1.61

TABLE II *(Continued)*

Inter.	0_t	XSS_t	$\Delta RR'_t$	η_{L_t}	Δr_{t-1}	Δdr_{t-1}	Δar_{t-1}	$IDRP_t$	$\bar{R}^2$ DW
1924-1929:									
79.9	-2.69	-23.76	.0179	15.79	33.48	-13.71	-30.62	-12.07	.60
(1.10)	(-2.76)	(-1.81)	(.50)	(1.68)	(3.51)	(-.88)	(-1.48)	(-2.94)	1.89
1924-1930:									
115.8	-2.78	-19.54	.0160	10.52	32.71	-10.29	-33.58	-11.31	.59
(1.97)	(-3.70)	(-1.91)	(.49)	(1.73)	(4.16)	(-.71)	(-1.90)	(-3.52)	1.91
1924-June 1931:									
113.1	-2.73	-19.14	.0148	10.60	32.02	-12.67	-31.91	-11.51	.58
(2.19)	(-3.83)	(-2.06)	(.45)	(1.76)	(4.37)	(-.93)	(-1.90)	(-3.75)	1.94

Notes: Figures in parentheses below the reported coefficients are the associated sample t statistics. As indicated in the text, some of the independent variables are combined by principal component analysis into one variable. This is the case for IDRP. Finally, the coefficient of determination $\bar{R}^2$ has been adjusted for degrees of freedom in each case.

The first two equations in Table II correspond to the division based on Strong's absence from his position that began in early 1928 (i.e., 1924-1927 and 1928-1931). The second pair of equations correspond to a division of the period based approximately on Strong's death (i.e., 1924-1928 and 1929-1931). These results provided support for the hypothesis of consistent behavior. Furthermore, in none of the divisions does r_{L_t} have the necessary negative sign for the acceptance of the hypothesis that Federal Reserve officials used open market operations to obtain a differential between short-term rates in New York and London that would reverse the net gold inflow of the United States. Domestic considerations, however, *do* appear to have been important; and Federal Reserve policy seems to have been consistent with respect to the domestic goals.

These conclusions are not clear-cut however. The equations for the later period of both divisions (1928-1931 and 1929-1931) contain some bothersome coefficients. These apparent discrepancies are very likely to be the result of statistical problems.

With one exception, the regression equation for 1928-1931 does not differ greatly from the results for 1924-1927 or for the whole period, 1924-1931 (compare equation [I.6.c] in Table I). The exception is the insignificance of the coefficient of XSS_t for the period 1928-1931. This is, of course, precisely the period in which stock market speculation should have been most important in determining Federal Reserve policy. This curious result is probably the consequence of the increased collinearity between O_t and XSS_t when the period under examination excludes the years 1924-1927 during which XSS_t was assigned a value of zero, as explained previously.[62] Since collinearity decreases the reliability of the estimated coefficients, the insignificance of the coefficient of XSS_t is likely to be the result of this collinearity and not of the unimportance of stock market speculation in open market operations in 1928-1931.[63]

The same argument is applied to the results of the regression for 1929-1931. While the results here do *not* support the hypothesis of countercyclical policy (based on the coefficient of O_t), it is believed that this, too, is a result of the collinearity between XSS_t and O_t. As may be seen from Table II, the coefficient of XSS_t becomes much larger (negatively) and the coefficient of O_t becomes positive. An examination of the relevant simple correlation coefficients suggests that these changes may not be reliable.[64] Furthermore, the regression for this period is based on observations for only three years.

The remaining three regressions reported in Table II tend to support the conclusions summarized above. In the regressions that begin in 1924 but end at different points (December, 1927, 1928, 1929, 1930, and 1931; and June, 1931), it is apparent that the coefficients of all the variables are remarkably stable in all important respects. And, judging by the adjusted coefficients of determination and the Durbin-Watson coefficients, they are all reasonably good fits.[65]

Based on the results of testing Model I, there appears to be little support for the hypothesis of inconsistent behavior. However, the results of the tests of Model II should be examined before a final conclusion is drawn.

Results of the Tests of Model II

Table III contains the regression results for the shortened forms of equations (II.10) - (II.12) of Model II (shortened by substituting r_{t-1} for B_{t-1}, dr_{t-1}, and ar_{t-1} in all equations; and $IDRP_t$ for Δar_t and Δdr_t in equation [II.10.a], as before). The criteria for rejecting the relevant null hypotheses are the same as stated for Model I.[66] The results of the sub-period analysis are also contained in Table III.

Many of the comments regarding the results of the regressions for Model I are also applicable here. These will not be repeated. The emphasis in the discussion of the regression equations contained in Table III is on the important similarities and differences between the two models.

As before, in the equation for open market operations (equation [II.10.a]) the coefficients of the variables relating to stock market speculation and the level of output indicate that the hypotheses of an anti-speculation and a countercyclical policy should be accepted. Likewise, the past rate of interest seems to have been an important determinant of open market operations. In the present formulation,

Table III
REGRESSION RESULTS FOR MODEL II (WITH SUB-PERIOD ANALYSIS)

Inter.	XSS_{t-1}	$\dot{SP}_t$	O_t	$\dot{P}_t$	r_{Lt}	BT_t	ΔG_{t-1}	G_{t-1}	ERS_t	DG_t	$\Delta RR'_t$ or ΔN_t	Δdr_{t-1}	Δar_{t-1}	$IDRP_t$	r_{t-1}		$\bar{R}^2$ DW	Equation Number
Open market operations (Equation II.10):																		
-383.5	-17.75	-1.69	-3.31	6.63	.956	.065	.117	.099	19.95	-3.05	.022	-2.74	-7.30	-6.29	53.30		.52	(II.10.a)
(-2.04)	(-1.76)	(-1.59)	(-3.65)	(1.14)	(.15)	(.60)	(1.51)	(2.73)	(.78)	(-.25)	(.62)	(-.18)	(-.41)	(-2.33)	(4.70)		2.04	
Changes in the discount rate (Equation II.11):														Δar_t		XDA_t		
-.499	.1635	.0215	.0079	-.0704	-.0257	-.0018	-.0011	.0033	-.2611	.0527	.0003	-.2465	.0096	.8896	-.0259	-.1901	.65	(II.11.a)
(-.35)	(2.03)	(2.83)	(1.18)	(-1.64)	(-.53)	(-2.30)	(-1.96)	(1.83)	(-1.39)	(.57)	(1.06)	(-2.07)	(.07)	(9.59)	(-.30)	(-1.52)	2.01	
Changes in the acceptance rate (Equation II.12):														Δdr_t				
2.964	-.0424	-.0119	.0045	.0502	.1010	.0010	.0011	-.0006	-.0986	-.1037	-.0001	.0504	.0300	.6004	-.2117		.71	(II.12.a)
(2.60)	(-.68)	(-1.84)	(.81)	(1.42)	(2.64)	(1.46)	(2.24)	(-2.72)	(-.63)	(-1.38)	(-.44)	(.53)	(.28)	(9.49)	(-3.12)		1.95	
Sub-Period analysis of open market operations:																		
1924-1927:																		
524.4	---	-2.19	-1.74	1.60	27.30	-.1003	.0869	.0934	-179.2	-45.43	.0169	-27.41	-5.62	-7.42	8.74		.50	
(1.16)		(-.63)	(-.98)	(.16)	(1.56)	(-.52)	(.40)	(1.57)	(-2.05)	(-1.84)	(.35)	(-.88)	(-.17)	(-1.08)	(.37)		2.47	
1928-1931:																		
-648.9	-16.75	-2.30	-3.75	6.94	-10.11	.0854	.1016	.1484	33.19	—	-.0147	1.11	16.23	-3.04	72.68		.55	
(-2.04)	(-.84)	(-1.71)	(-2.69)	(.68)	(-.89)	(.44)	(.95)	1.98)	(.91)		(-.25)	(.06)	(.57)	(-.92)	(3.50)		1.69	
1924-1928:																		
186.2	17.85	-4.96	-2.66	11.72	29.95	.0492	.358	.0757	-94.47	-29.54	.0131	3.18	-34.01	-6.30	28.83		.55	
(.46)	(.47)	(-1.79)	(-1.71)	(1.43)	(1.92)	(.31)	(2.14)	(1.37)	(-1.22)	(-1.37)	(.29)	(.12)	(-1.09)	(-1.09)	(-1.53)		2.20	
1929-1931:																		
-894.1	-30.96	-2.35	-3.00	16.00	-15.21	.0467	.040	.1975	29.72	—	.0669	-11.57	26.74	-4.13	77.01		.63	
(-2.95)	(-1.36)	(-1.92)	(-1.92)	(1.49)	(-1.37)	(.23)	(.36)	(2.57)	(.89)		(1.06)	(-.65)	(.93)	(1.39)	(3.45)		2.13	
1924-June 1931:																		
229.6	-22.17	-3.13	-2.44	10.05	10.98	.1132	.2206	.0330	-73.46	-34.67	-.0182	-2.53	-29.36	-9.40	32.43		.62	
(1.03)	(-2.09)	(-2.95)	(-2.62)	(1.81)	(1.60)	(1.11)	(1.81)	(.89)	(-1.40)	(-1.95)	(-.52)	(-.18)	(-1.68)	(-2.82)	(2.74)		2.15	

Notes: Figures in parentheses below the reported coefficients are the associated sample t statistics. As indicated in the text, some of the independent variables are combined by principal component analysis into one variable. This is the case for IDRP. Finally, the coefficient of determination $\bar{R}^2$ has been adjusted for degrees of freedom in each case.

however, there appears to be some support for Wicker's international theory not apparent before.

In equation (II.10.a), the coefficients of ΔG_{t-1} and G_{t-1}, the first difference and the level of the United States monetary gold stock in the previous month, support the hypothesis that the Fed used open market operations to reverse the inflow of gold. The positive coefficients of both ΔG_{t-1} and G_{t-1} imply that open market purchases were greater the greater the gold inflow and the greater the stock of monetary gold. This is, of course, counter to the sterilization of gold flows which is supposed to have taken place (and which would be evident in the coefficient of $\Delta RR'_t$). While none of the other "international" variables support the international theory, the support of these two variables is noteworthy.

The regression for changes in the discount rate (equation [II.11.a]) provides mixed results. As before, the stock market appears to have been an important consideration, while the coefficient of output does not support the countercyclical theory. The "international" variables are divided between support and non-support. The coefficients of BT_t and ΔG_{t-1} have the expected signs if the international theory is correct, but the other relevant coefficients do not support the theory. One of these other coefficients, the coefficient of ERS_t, has the "wrong" sign—it indicates a policy hostile to the policy prescribed for a return to gold.

Equation (II.12.a) for changes in the acceptance rate provides results similar to the results of Model I. Again, the coefficients of the speculation variables (XSS_{t-1} and $\dot{SP}_t$) do not support the hypothesis that changes in the acceptance rate were used to stop stock market speculation. This time, the coefficient of output also fades into insignificance. With respect to the international theory, the coefficients of ${}^{r}L_t$ (as before), G_{t-1}, and DG_t (the dummy variable for the period prior to Britain's return to gold) provide support for the "return-to-gold" theory, although BT_t and ΔG_{t-1} have the "wrong" signs.

What, then, can be said about Federal Reserve behavior during this period? The results are mixed, and this makes the interpretation difficult. But it would appear from equation (II.10.a) that *both* domestic and international considerations were important to some extent in the

TABLE IV

Beta Coefficients for Selected Variables from Regression Equations (II.10.a) - (II.12.a)

Dependent	Independent Variable										
Variable	XSS_{t-1}	$\dot{SP}_t$	0_t	r_{L_t}	BT_t	ΔG_{t-1}	G_{t-1}	ERS_t	DG_t	r_{t-1}	XDA_t
$\Delta GS'_t$	-.21	-.18	-.99	--a	--a	.19	.44	--a	--a	1.34	--c
Δdr_t	.22	.27	--a	--a	-.18	-.21	--a	-.19	--a	--a	-.12
Δar_t	--a	--b	--a	.31	.11	.21	-.34	--a	-.12	-.68	--c

[a] These coefficients are not reported because of the statistical insignificance of the corresponding regression coefficients.

[b] This coefficient is not reported because of a “wrong” sign.

[c] This variable is not included in this equation.

determination of open market policy. Which was more important? As previously indicated, this is a question that could be better answered if it were possible to solve equation (II.10.a) for the weights attached to each of the goals in the disutility function (II.1). Since this is not possible, it is necessary to work with the coefficients of equation (II.10.a) which contain not only these weights, but also the parameters of the structural and behavioral equations of the model.

The coefficients themselves cannot be compared to answer the question of relative importance because these coefficients are influenced by the units involved. An associated statistic, the beta coefficient, is free of this influence, however. It can therefore be used to compare the relative importance of fluctuations in the independent variables in explaining fluctuations in the dependent variable.[67]

The beta coefficients of selected variables for equations (II.10.a) - (II.12.a) are reported in Table IV. A brief analysis of these coefficients will provide *some* evidence on the relative importance of the "domestic" versus the "international" variables.

In the case of open market operations, it is evident that the most important variable is the lagged value of the interest rate. This, of course, provides no evidence on the question of domestic versus international goals since the prior state of the market would be important regardless of whether the goals were international or domestic. However, the second most important variable is output. This might indicate that the domestic goal was of primary importance. The lagged level of the gold stock is less important than output, but apparently more so than the remaining variables which appear to be approximately equally important. The conclusion is, therefore, that the goal of stabilization of output would seem to be the most important since the fluctuations in output are most important by this test.[68]

The beta coefficients for the explanatory variables in the equation for changes in the discount rate are not very helpful since they are virtually indistinguishable.[69] It is interesting only to note that the beta coefficient for ERS_t, which has the wrong sign from the pro-return-to-gold theory, is of equal importance to the coefficients of BT_t and ΔG_{t-1}, which have the appropriate signs.

Finally, since the domestic goals do not appear to be supported in equation (II.12.a), only the international goals affect changes in acceptance rate. The relative importance of r_{L_t} and G_{t-1} seems to be somewhat greater than that of the other "international" variables. Since these two variables and DGt (the dummy variable) have the appropriate sign for the pro-return-to-gold theory, it is perhaps safe to conclude that the net result is in favor of the international theory.[70]

The results of the tests of Model II seem to confirm the results of the tests of Model I except that the "international" theory is given added support. This is perhaps due to the more complete specification of Model II. It does seem apparent that if Federal Reserve policy was designed to support the return of the world to the gold standard by decreasing short-term interest rates at home relative to their levels abroad, this policy was probably implemented more by changes in policy rates than by open market operations. This is perhaps logical since these rates *may* have been thought to more directly influence New York short term rates,[71] and since these two rates were more directly under the control of Benjamin Strong, and later, George Harrison, both of whom apparently supported the need for a world-wide return to, and continuing support of, the gold standard.

Before proceeding to the results of the bi-period analysis, it is interesting to note a difference between the regressions for changes in the discount and acceptance rates that is perhaps important in explaining the difference between the way in which the two rates were viewed by Federal Reserve officials. One of these differences has been previously noted—changes in the discount rate were positively related to both XSS_{t-1} and $\dot{SP}_t$. This is the result that would be expected under the hypothesis that changes in this rate were, in part, intended to stop stock market speculation. But changes in the acceptance rate were either not related to stock market speculation or were intended to encourage this speculation. Since the latter conclusion seems unlikely, it seems safe to favor the former conclusion.

Why should changes in the discount and acceptance rates not *both* be related to stock market speculation? The answer could be that Fed officials did not believe that credit extended through the purchases of acceptances would find its way into the stock market. This being the case, there was no need or reason to raise acceptance rates in response to stock market speculation. Keeping the acceptance rate relatively low may have been the way Fed officials hoped to satisfy "legitimate" business needs while choking off credit to the stock market. This is the "real bills" doctrine applied to acceptances rather than discounts. It was accepted by the officials of the New York Reserve Bank, if not by all the Federal Reserve officials, that the credit extended through discounts could support stock market speculation. Perhaps they did not think that credit extended through the purchase of acceptances could likewise support such speculation.[72]

The other difference between the regressions for Δdr_t and Δar_t has not been previously noted. Based on equation (II.11.a) it would appear that changes in the discount rate were negatively related to the "expected" increase in prices, i.e., that such changes promoted inflation. On the other hand, the apparent response of the Fed to expected inflation was to increase the acceptance rate, i.e., that changes in the acceptance rate worked against inflation. The difference could be a statistical accident, or it could reflect an actual difference. While it seems unlikely that Federal Reserve policy was designed to promote inflation in any way,[73] it could well be that the acceptance rate was the principal instrument they used in combating it.

Recalling the development of Model II, the expected positive sign on the coefficient of $\dot{P}_t$ was based on the belief that an expectation of rising prices would encourage commodity speculation. While there is no evidence that such speculation occurred in this period or that the Fed was concerned about combating inflation, if the officials felt that such a result was likely, they may well have responded in the first instance by raising acceptance rates since acceptances were used in part to finance the carrying of inventories. In other words, the positive coefficient of $\dot{P}_t$ in the regression equation for Δar_t, and its insignificance elsewhere, has a sound justification.

The differences between the two rate equations therefore have a reasonable explanation: changes in the acceptance rate were employed to do what they could best do—to discourage possible commodity speculation; changes in the discount rate were employed to discourage stock market speculation. This could be true because of the belief that Federal Reserve credit extended through discounting entered directly the pool of available credit for all purposes while the extension of credit by the purchase of acceptances went directly to finance international trade and domestic accumulation of inventories.

The bi-period analysis for open market operations under Model II is also contained in Table III. The results of this analysis, as with Model I, are interpreted as supporting the hypothesis of consistent behavior, although with two possible exceptions. The two expections are (1) the possibility that international considerations *were* more important prior to 1928 and (2) the possibility of "over-reaction" to the low rates of 1930-1931.

The regression for open market operations in the years 1924-1927 provides the interesting result, if interpreted on its appearance in Table III, that domestic goals were *not* important, while the promotion of the return of the world (by way of Britain) to gold, *was* important. The coefficient of O_t does not support the hypothesis of a countercyclical policy. But the coefficients of G_{t-1} and, now, ERS_t *do* support the return-to-gold theory. The result must be tempered however by the totally unexpected negative sign on DG_t and by the realization, again, of multicollinearity.[74]

The other possible exception to the consistency of Federal Reserve behavior is the considerable increase (absolutely) in the coefficient of r_{t-1} in the period of 1928-1931 over the period 1924-1927, and again in the period 1929-1931 over the period 1924-1928. This suggests that Federal Reserve officials may have "over-reacted" to the unprecedentedly low rates of 1930-1931 and therefore not have purchased as large a quantity of securities as they would otherwise have done.

With these two possible exceptions, the regressions for the different periods presented in Table III seem to be fairly stable and to support the previous conclusion that open market operations were primarily intended to help obtain certain domestic goals. Nevertheless, the hypothesis that international goals were of greater importance before 1928 than after, as is the implication of the study by Clarke, cannot be entirely rejected. Whether or not this was related to the increasing illness and death of Benjamin Strong can only be supposition.[75]

Further Results and a Comment on Alternative Formulations

One of the problems with the results for both models is that the inclusion of Δar_t in the equation explaining Δdr_t, and vice-versa, confuses the results. However, exclusion of these variables would not be acceptable because this would probably be a misspecification of the equations: changes in the discount (acceptance) rate probably were dependent on the concurrent changes in the acceptance (discount) rate. The reason has been referred to before—a probable desire to keep the rates in line with each other, ceteris paribus.

In an effort to clarify the determinants of changes in both rates, the first principal component of Δdr_t and Δar_t, $IDRP_t$, was regressed on the variables entering the rate-change functions for both models. Then, in an effort to clarify the different forces in setting each rate, the change in the discount rate was regressed on the change in the acceptance rate plus the variables that are thought to distinguish between the changes. The results are reported below: with the t statistics, adjusted R^2, and Durbin-Watson statistics reported as before.

$$(1)\quad IDRP_t = \underset{(-1.07)}{-1.474} + \underset{(2.38)}{.970XSS_t} + \underset{(1.66)}{.030\,O_t} + \underset{(4.31)}{.746\,r_{L_t}}$$

$$+\underset{(.70)}{.0009\Delta N_t} \underset{(-1.74)}{-1.095\,\Delta dr_{t-1}} + \underset{(1.22)}{.885\,\Delta ar_{t-1}}$$

$$\underset{(-4.47)}{-\,1.155\,r_{t-1}} \underset{(-.97)}{-\,.683\,XDA_t} \qquad \bar{R}^2 = .28 \quad DW = 1.91$$

$$(2)\quad IDRP_t = \underset{(2.85)}{21.66} + \underset{(1.25)}{.568\,XSS_t} + \underset{(1.22)}{.052\,\dot{SP}_t} + \underset{(2.72)}{.098\,O_t}$$

$$\underset{(-.11)}{-\,.026\,\dot{P}_t} + \underset{(2.63)}{.674\,r_{L_t}} \underset{(-.99)}{-\,.004\,BT_t} + \underset{(.08)}{.003\,\Delta G_{t-1}}$$

$$-\,.003\,G_{t-1} - 2.88\,ERS_t - .622DG_t + .001\,\Delta N_t$$

$$(-1.93) \quad (-2.82) \quad (-1.22) \quad (.79)$$

$$- 1.105\ \Delta dr_{t-1} - .071\ \Delta ar_{t-1} - 2.041 r_{t-1}$$
$$(-1.66) \quad (-.09) \quad (-4.78)$$

$$- .314\ XDA_t \qquad \bar{R}^2 = .34$$
$$(-.45) \qquad DW = 1.82$$

$$(3) \quad \Delta dr_t = -.017 + .897\ \Delta ar_t + .114\ XSS_t$$
$$(-.73) \quad (13.19) \quad (2.15)$$

$$- .225\ XDA_t \qquad \bar{R}^2 = .65$$
$$(-1.98) \qquad DW = 2.14$$

Equation (1) and (2) are based on Models I and II respectively with all of the variables included that enter either or both of equations (I.7) and (I.8) or (II.11) and (II.12). The expected signs can be obtained by examining any of these last equations.

Equation (1) supports both the international and domestic theories. According to equation (1), the common fluctuations in Δdr_t and Δar_t are explained by the Fed's efforts to stop stock market speculation, stabilize output, *and* obtain a rate differential between New York and London which would reverse the gold inflow. With respect to the question of relative importance, the beta coefficients may again be used. The relevant coefficients are -.83 for r_{t-1}, .51 for r_{L_t}, .33 for XSS_t, and .26 for O_t. It would appear, then, from this result, that the international goal may have been slightly more important than the domestic goals.

Equation (2) provides somewhat different results. In this case, the coefficients of XSS_t and $\dot{SP}_t$ do not support the hypothesis that rate changes were used to discourage stock market speculation (by the same criteria as applied throughout this study). The coefficient of output indicates a counter cyclical policy, while the coefficients of r_{L_t} and G_{t-1} support the return-to-gold theory. The coefficient of ERS_t, however, has the wrong sign for support of this theory.

The Beta coefficients are -1.46 for r_{t-1}, .83 for O_t, -.51 for ERS_t, .46 for r_{L_t}, and -.36 for G_{t-1}. Based on these coefficients, it would appear that the domestic goal of stabilization of output was more important than the international goal.

Finally, equation (3) is the result of the attempt to determine the difference between the factors influencing changes in the discount and acceptance rates. It was noted in the results of testing both models that changes in the discount rate were related to the stock market while changes in the acceptance rate were not. In addition, the dummy variable XDA applies specifically to changes in the discount rate.

Therefore, equation (3) was run to test the hypothesis that the factors influencing Δdr alone were the stock market and the dummy variable for direct action, and that, abstracting from these variables, changes in the discount rate would be the same as changes in the acceptance rate. Equation (3) seems to lend support to this idea.[76]

Finally, regressions were run similar to those reported in Tables I and III for changes in the discount and acceptance rates except that they included the current changes in the prime commercial rate and the open market acceptance rate, respectively, in place of the independent variables Δar_t and Δdr_t, respectively. These regressions are not reported here because they do not add to what has been said before. They are mentioned, however, for the sake of completeness *and* because changes in the acceptance rate at the New York Fed can be almost entirely explained by changes in the open market rate on acceptances alone. The simple correlation coefficient between these two variables is .85. This could have been predicted on the basis of Burgess's description of the acceptance rate. According to Burgess,

> . . . the fixing of the price for buying bills is much less a matter of policy than the fixing of the discount rate for loans. The buying rate for bills follows very closely the open-market rates for bills and does not ordinarily reflect judgement as to the general credit situation.[77]

What, then, explains the results obtained in the tests of both Models I and II? It was changes in acceptance rate rather than the discount rate that appeared to be more closely related to the target variables. This result was probably the result of the fact that changes in the discount rate came in steps while changes in the acceptance rate were generally smoother. And, if the acceptance rate generally followed the open market rate on acceptances, and if the latter responded promptly to supply and demand conditions for credit, then Δar_t could be expected to behave like a policy variable even if it were not. Finally, the above statement by Burgess certainly does not exclude the possibility that changes in the acceptance rate were at least sometimes used to effect Federal Reserve policy.

It would appear, based on all the evidence, that Federal Reserve rate policy, meaning changes in both of these rates, was used to achieve both international and domestic goals. While changes in the acceptance rate may have been more of an automatic adjustment to market conditions, they were probably used at times to tighten or ease credit conditions generally. It is fairly clear, however, that only the discount rate was used to discourage stock market speculation.

In addition to these results for the discount and acceptance rates, further results were also obtained for open market operations. It was noted previously that similar results were obtained regardless of exactly how the open market purchases and sale of securities were defined. The regression reported below using ΔGS (changes in the average daily holdings of all classes of government securities) instead of $\Delta GS'$ illustrates this point.

(4) $\Delta GS_t = 117.8 - 2.62\, O_t - 13.51\, XSSt$
(3.26) (-5.32) (-1.39)

$+ .077\, \Delta RR'_t + 10.57\, r_{L_t} - 13.94\, \Delta dr_{t-1} - 36.33\, \Delta ar_{t-1}$
(2.08) (2.11) (-.89) (-2.04)

$- 9.65\, IDRP_t + 26.30 r_{t-1} + 34.94\, XM + 18.41\, XJ$
(-3.48) (3.51) (3.03) (1.54)

$+21.51\, XS + 13.88\, XD$ $\bar{R}^2 = .53$
(1.85) (1.14) $DW = 1.76$

In this equation, XM, XJ, XS, and XD, are dummy variables for the months of March, June, September, and December, that is, the months during which Treasury operations usually took place. The coefficients of these variables have the expected positive signs.

A comparison of equation (4) with equation (I.6.c) in Table I reveals that the results are virtually the same with respect to the common variables. Apparently the use of $\Delta GS'_t$ (as previously defined) did not influence the results.

Finally, as previously stated, an independent check on the definition of $\Delta RR'_t$ seemed desirable. Several alternatives were tried. The regression reported below used separate changes in the gold stock (ΔG_t), acceptances (ΔA_t), currency in circulation (ΔM_t), and a residual change (ΔRR_t) representing the change in the sum of all other sources less uses.

$$
\begin{aligned}
(5)\quad \Delta GS'_t = {} & \underset{(3.38)}{117.4} - \underset{(-5.26)}{2.50\, O_t} - \underset{(-1.64)}{15.62\, XSS_t} + \underset{(1.27)}{6.11\, r_{L_t}} \\
& - \underset{(-.90)}{13.01\, \Delta dr_{t-1}} - \underset{(-1.45)}{24.62\, \Delta ar_{t-1}} - \underset{(-3.90)}{12.34\, IDRP_t} \\
& + \underset{(4.05)}{29.62\, r_{t-1}} + \underset{(.96)}{.061\, \Delta A_t} - \underset{(-.92)}{.071\, \Delta G_t} \\
& + \underset{(1.13)}{.046\, \Delta M_t} - \underset{(-1.35)}{.219\, \Delta RR_t} \qquad R^2 = .50 \quad DW = 1.90
\end{aligned}
$$

A comparison of equation (5) with equation (I.6.c) of Table I indicates, again, that the results are basically the same. Even in the form above, it appears that defensive operations were minimal, if they existed at all.

Before concluding this chapter, it seems advisable to mention some of the alternative formulations with which experiments were conducted. These included formulations based on the *levels* of the discount and acceptance rates, formulations utilizing first differences throughout (dependent and independent variables), and formulations with other variables. Of particular interest in the last category were experiments with an independent variable representing the difference between short-term rates in New York and London. In none of these alternatives were results obtained that were substantially different from those reported above.

It appears to be unlikely that the results are radically influenced by the precise formulation of the underlying model assumed to be utilized by Fed officials, provided only that the model is similar in its main elements to the ones employed here.[78]

Conclusions

The empirical tests of the hypotheses described in Chapter Two have provided significant evidence on the validity of these hypotheses although the evidence has not always been conclusive. The conclusions drawn from the tests are summarized here.

There appears to be no evidence to support Wicker's contention that the primary goal of Federal Reserve policy in this period was the return of the gold standard and the maintenance of same. Open market operations were apparently used primarily to stabilize output and to attempt to stop the growing speculation in the stock market. While there is some evidence that the international motive was present, there is certainly no basis in the data for the conclusion that it was the most important objective.

To the extent that the goal of reducing gold flows to the United States by lowering domestic short-term rates played a part in Federal Reserve decisions, it appears to have been more important in the setting of discount and acceptance rates than in open market operations of the System. This could easily be the result of the more direct control of the discount and acceptance rates by Benjamin Strong and his successor George Harrison.

While the evidence seems to favor the conclusion that Federal Reserve behavior was consistent before and after 1929, the hypothesis that the international goals were more important in open market operations before 1928 than after cannot be completely rejected. The empirical tests do not provide a clear-cut answer to this question.

Why, then, did the Fed not pursue large scale purchases during 1930? The answer, based on all of the available evidence, seems to have several parts. One problem was the apparent fear of stimulating a renewed speculative expansion on the stock market. In addition, as Brunner and Meltzer have suggested, it appears that Fed officials viewed the relatively low and declining short-term rate for credit as an indicator that the market was already "easy." There is some evidence that the Fed "over-reacted" to these low rates in comparison with their behavior earlier in the period. This is probably to be expected since these officials had not dealt with a similar situation before. This inexperience combined with the doubt expressed by some of the officials of the efficacy of large-scale purchases in reviving the economy also contribute to the explanation of their failure to respond with the kind of purchases necessary.[79]

It seems reasonable to conclude that the failure of the Federal Reserve to undertake large scale purchases after 1929 can be explained without resort to the theory of a radical departure from pre-1929 behavior. The empirical evidence certainly provides little support for the latter explanation.

One of the surprising aspects of the results of both models is the apparent absence of defensive operations—operations designed to protect member bank reserves from external changes. This is in sharp contrast to conclusions of studies of later periods.[80] This is very likely the result of an important difference between the period of 1924-1931 and later years. This difference is in the existence of a large acceptance market in the earlier period which ceased to be important in the mid-1930's.[81] It is probably true that in the period under examination member banks themselves provided for defensive operations by adjusting the volume of acceptances offered to the Federal Reserve Banks to changes in the gold stock, currency in circulation, and so forth. Evidence in support of this theory is presented in Appendix B.[82] Therefore, the failure of the regression analysis to indicate the importance of defensive operations is probably the result of the use of acceptances in defensive operations, not government securities.

What conclusions can be drawn regarding the use of the short-sighted model (Model I) versus the model in which the ultimate target variables were used (Model II)? The latter model appears to provide a slightly better fit, but this difference is negligible. The most important difference between the two is the support given by Model II

7. Having traced through the effects of purchases and sales of government securities on short-term credit, Burgess states:

> One is tempted to try to trace further the causal relationship between open-market operations and the condition of business, commodity prices, movement of the stock market, and so forth, but clearly the experience in these matters has covered too brief a time to make possible any safe generalizations.

Burgess, *Federal Reserve Policy and Benjamin Strong*, p. 224.

8. Ibid., pp. 275-276.

9. Brunner and Meltzer, "What Did We Learn?" pp. 341-348.

10. Wicker, "A Reinterpretation," pp. 329-332.

11. As should be clear when the model is developed later, the resulting reduced-form equation for purchases and sales of government securities would be the same in all important respects whether the variable entering the disutility function is the short-term rate of interest or borrowings. The interest rate is used because this allows for the effects of the discount and acceptance rates on the credit market, and this permits the solution of the same disutility function for all three policy variables.

12. Wood, *Federal Reserve Behavior*, p. 149.

13. See n. 7.

14. For example, the stabilization hearings before the House Committee on Banking and Currency were held in 1926 and 1927. See Hardy, *Credit Policies*, pp. 199-202.

15. Burgess, *Federal Reserve Policy and Benjamin Strong*, p. 203.

16. See the *Tenth Annual Report*, pp. 4-5. The lag may well be too short, but this probably is of little consequence.

17. That this is true may be seen by considering the case of B_t and B_{t-1}.

$$-b_2B_t - b_3B_{t-1} = -b_2(B_{t-1} + \Delta B_t) - b_3B_{t-1}$$
$$= -b_2\Delta B_t - (b_2 + b_3)B_{t-1}$$
$$= -b_2\Delta B_t - b'_3 B_{t-1}$$

where $b'_3 = b_2 + b_3$. Likewise, $b'_5 = b_4 + b_5$, and $b'_7 = b_6 + b_7$.

18. See n. 16.

19. We have

$$\Delta N_t \equiv \Delta RR_t - \Delta S_t{}^B + \Delta U_t{}^R$$

From the reserve equation, we also have

$$\Delta B_t = \Delta R_t - \Delta S_t{}^B + \Delta U_t{}^R$$
$$\Delta B_t - \Delta R_t = - \Delta S_t{}^B + \Delta U_t{}^R$$

Therefore,

$$\Delta N_t = \Delta RR_t + \Delta B_t - \Delta R_t$$
$$= \Delta B_t - \Delta ER_t$$

since the change in excess reserves is equal to the change in total reserves less the change in required reserves.

20. Clarke, *Central Bank Cooperation*, pp. 34-35.

21. Wicker, "A Reinterpretation," pp. 333, 336. Clarke, *Central Bank Cooperation*, pp. 85-96, pp. 124-127. *Excerpts*. p. 130.

22. There is one difference between the two cases, however. A rise in the discount rate will serve to lower borrowings in the next period whereas a rise in the acceptance rate will serve to increase borrowings. This is not explicitly taken into account in the coefficients of Δdr_t and Δar_t in equation (I.6), but it may have influenced the thinking of the policy makers.

23. Wood, *Federal Reserve Behavior*, pp. 140-141. The practical reason for the inclusion of the lagged values of the target variables is so that the target variables will appear in the final equation for Federal Reserve behavior (in lagged form, of course). If the lagged values were not included, then the target variable would not appear in the results because of the substitution of the equations explaining the target variables themselves. (This is not made clear in Wood's exposition.)

24. Clarke, *Central Bank Cooperation*, pp. 34-35.

25. Since the parity rate was a constant, from a statistical point of view, it is unnecessary to actually take the difference between the current exchange rate and the parity rate.

26. Clarke, *Central Bank Cooperation*, pp. 124-129.

27. "If the present high interest rates are continued for several months, it seems probable that business activity may be affected six months or a year from now." Memorandum of Acting Chairman, July 18, 1928, in *Excerpts*, p. 218.

28. *Tenth Annual Report*, pp. 4-5.

29. See, for example, Clay J. Anderson, *Money Market Conditions*, pp. 51-52, or Hardy, *Credit Policies*, pp. 37-40, for a history of this early period.

30. U.S. Board of Governors, *Nineteenth Annual Report* (Washington, DC: U.S. Government Printing Office, 1933), pp. 16-19.

31. Friedman and Schwartz, *Monetary History*, pp. 322-323.

32. The Reconstruction Finance Corporation also began operations early that year to provide emergency aid to ailing financial institutions. It is not clear whether this did or did not affect Federal Reserve behavior.

33. Average daily holdings of excess reserves by member banks reached $526 million dollars in December, 1932. Prior to 1932, excess reserves had rarely exceeded $100 million dollars and were largely ignored by Fed officials. See *Banking and Monetary Statistics*, pp. 370-371; and Burgess, *Federal Reserve Policy and Benjamin Strong*, pp. 115-119.

34. Burgess concludes that excess reserves, at least for New York member banks, were low and showed little fluctuation during this period. That is, his observations support the statement in the text. It is not as important that excess reserves did or did not actually fluctuate as it is that Fed officials did or did not *think* they did, for it is what the policy makers *believed* to be reality that entered their decision process. Apparently, Fed officials (at least Burgess) felt excess reserves could be ignored. See Burgess *Federal Reserve Policy and Benjamin Strong*, pp. 115-119.

35. Previously, we derived the definition

$$\Delta N_t = \Delta B_t - \Delta ER_t$$

(See n. 19). If the change in excess reserves is zero, then it must be true that the change in reserves is exactly equal to the change in *required* reserves. In this case, the change in member bank borrowings takes place to provide for any change in required reserves that is not provided for by changes in other sources or uses of reserve funds.

It should be noted, however, that this does not exclude the possibility of member banks' changing loans and investments in order to change their required reserves. In the first instance, they are forced to borrow. Given time, however, they can adjust their portfolio position.

36. *Excerpts*, pp. 8, 147, 186.

37. The statement comes after reference to the rapid increase in brokers' loans and stock prices from July-November, 1927. Strong said

> It is clear from a study of such relationships as those of stock yields with bond yields and with money rates, that

> the current level of stock market prices is less abnormal than a casual inspection of prices alone would suggest.

Strong memorandum to Board, November 2, 1927, in *Excerpts*, p. 147.

38. This analysis is oversimplified in ignoring other investment opportunities. But it is probably fair to assume a greater substitutability between stocks and bonds than between either of these and, say, real estate.

39. This should not be interpreted to mean that this differential would at *all times* be a good measure of speculative activity in stocks. The differential is thought to be a good measure of speculation for years in which it is used only. It is, in any case, what Federal Reserve officials *believed* to be an indicator of speculation that is important.

40. The available data appear to have been limited to an index of department store stocks compiled by the Federal Reserve and several indices of commodity stocks of both manufactured and raw materials compiled by the United States Department of Commerce. For a brief description of these indices see Donald H. Davenport and Frances V. Scott, *An Index to Business Indices* (Chicago: Business Publications, Inc., 1937), pp. 139, 146. This volume was very helpful in determining the availability of data for several variables.

41. The indices mentioned in n. 40 were tried in several combinations. Among these were the ratio of the index of department store stocks to the index of department store sales, the combined index of commodity stocks (alone and as a ratio to industrial production), and the cumulative sum of the change in the ratio of commodity stocks to industrial production from the last trough in business activity. The last indicator was used in an attempt to bypass the problem of inventory accumulation during recession.

42. This may have been the result of successful Federal Reserve policy; that is, the Fed may have successfully avoided commodity

speculation by pursuing a policy of tightening credit before such speculation had a chance to occur. Or it could, of course, be simply the result of some unspecified factors affecting the desire to accumulate inventories.

43. The weights used were four, two, and one, so that, for example,

$$\dot{P} = \frac{4\frac{\Delta P}{P_{t-1}} + 2\frac{\Delta P}{P}_{t-2} + 1\frac{\Delta P}{P_{t-3}}}{7}$$

where P is the wholesale price index. There are countless other possibilities; none of them are completely satisfactory since it is difficult to define people's expectations. The present formulation is appealing because it takes account of values in the recent past but with declining importance attached to values farther in the past.

44. All changes are taken to be changes in the average daily holdings from one month to the next.

45. For a full account of these operations, see either Burgess, *Federal Reserve Policy and Benjamin Strong*, pp. 99-103, or Hardy, *Credit Policies*, pp. 68-69.

46. *Excerpts*, pp. 13-14, 17, 45.

47. Burgess, *Federal Reserve Policy and Benjamin Strong*, pp. 107-108, 208-209.

48. Ibid., p. 209.

49. In addition, similar operations occurred in months other than March, June, September, and December in two of the years used in the tests (1927 and 1928). See U.S. Federal Reserve Board, *Seventeenth Annual Report* (Washington, DC: U.S. Government Printing Office, 1931), pp. 52-53.

50. It has been suggested by Professor Anthony Tang that it would be more appropriate to use the data actually available to the Fed at the

time they made their decisions rather than use later, revised versions of the same series. In many cases, this is not a factor. But it *could* be important in a series such as industrial production.

However, it appeared to me from a brief examination of the relevant data that such revised series are not much changed from the original data; and revised data (as of 1931-1932) are used. Since the revised data are based largely on information available at the time the data were first generated, the difference between the revised and original data should not be of great importance.

51. E. Malinvaud, *Statistical Methods of Econometrics*, Studies in Mathematical and Managerial Economics, Vol. 6 (Amsterdam: North-Holland Publishing Company, 1966. Chicago: Rand McNally and Company, 1966), pp. 608-609.

52. IMC_{t-1} accounts for 93 percent of the common variation of B_{t-1}, dr_{t-1}, and ar_{t-1}; $IDRP_t$ accounts for 89 percent of the common variation of Δdr_t and Δar_t.

53. The corresponding values for an alpha of .05 are 1.66 and -1.66. I have chosen a larger alpha because some of the variables are at best incomplete proxies for the true variable we would like to have. An example that is directly affected by the alpha level chosen is the variable for stock market speculation, XSS. Because the actual variable used is only a rough approximation of a true measure of the existence and magnitude of stock market speculation, I am willing to accept the alternative hypothesis on the basis of weaker evidence than might otherwise be the case.

Furthermore, the regression is being fitted to monthly data, which exhibit much more random variation than do, say, quarterly data. The spectral analysis of ΔGS and ΔGS' in Appendix B indicates the existence of considerable noise, or random variation, in the policy variable. This, too, is a reason for accepting weaker evidence of a true relation, since the true relation is difficult to capture.

54. Burgess, for example, says that discount rate changes and open market operations usually ". . . supplement each other." (Burgess,

Federal Reserve Policy and Benjamin Strong, p. 224.) He goes on to describe how the two can be used, and had been used, in complementary fashion. (Ibid, pp. 224-225).

55. See, for example, Burgess, *Federal Reserve Policy and Benjamin Strong*, pp. 191-193, 208. It is interesting to note that, in equations (I.7.a) and (I.8.a) where the lagged values of member bank borrowings, the discount rate, and the acceptance rate are not replaced by either their first principal component or the market rate of interest, the lagged value of the "dependent" rate has a negative sign while the lagged value of the "other" rate has a positive sign. This tends to support the idea that it was the desire of policy makers to keep these two rates together, ceteris paribus.

56. More precisely, the variable assumes a value of one for February-June inclusive. While the discount rate at the New York Reserve Bank was not finally raised until August, 1929, Hardy concludes that the policy itself was virtually abandoned by June, 1929. (Hardy, *Credit Policies*, p. 138.) Experiments show that the coefficient of XDA is not substantially changed whether the period of direct action is considered ended in June or July.

57. The statistical reason for the insignificance of most of the coefficients in the discount rate equation is the overwhelming influence of Δar_t. Many of the other variables which are collinear with Δar_t are "robbed" of their significance. More is said on this point in the "further results" reported below.

58. The critical t values for the different periods at the .10 level are as follows: 1924-1927 and 1928-1931, t = 1.30 or -1.30; 1929-1931, t = 1.31 or -1.31. All others are either t = 1.29 or -1.29 or t = 1.30 or -1.30.

59. Friedman and Schwartz, *Monetary History*, pp. 407-419.

60. The appropriate references and a thorough description of the Friedman-Schwartz hypothesis may be found in Chapter Two.

61. Clarke, *Central Bank Cooperation*, pp. 141-142, 151-160. Again, a complete description of the point may be found in Chapter Two.

62. This point is illustrated by an examination of the relevant simple correlation coefficients:

	Simple Correlation Coefficients Between		
Period	XSS_t & O_t	XSS_t & $\Delta GS'_t$	O_t & $\Delta GS'_t$
1924-1931	.63	-.14	-.24
1928-1931	.83	-.16	-.17

As may be seen, the sample correlation between XSS_t and O_t increases when the period 1924-1927 is omitted.

63. This apparent rejection of the statistical results should not be taken to indicate a distrust of *all* the results summarized in this thesis. It is my intention not to reject the statistical results, but to carefully interpret and evaluate them. I do not believe that the statistical results can, or should, stand alone any more than I believe that the statements of the policy makers can, or should stand alone. Rather, it is to be desired that *all* of the evidence should be weighed and evaluated.

The opinion expressed in the text is based on (1) the fact that a considerable amount of time and attention was devoted by policy makers to the stock market in the years 1928-1930 and (2) the possibility of unreliable statistical results as outlined in the text. As a result, it is my opinion that stock market speculation was indeed very important in the determination of open market policy in this period.

64. The following table illustrates the point:

Period	Simple Correlation Coefficients Between XSS_t & O_t	XSS_t & $\Delta GS'_t$	O_t & $\Delta GS'_t$
1924-1931	.63	-.14	-.23
1928-1931	.89	-.31	-.05

In the later period, XSS_t could easily be statistically "robbing" O_t of some of its influence.

65. In each of these regressions, with the exception of the entire period, the hypothesis of a serially correlated error term can be rejected at the 95 percent level. This is not true of the regressions restricted to 1928-1931 and 1929-1931 or of the regression for the whole period. In these three cases, the results are indecisive.

66. Since there are more variables in the equations of Model II than in the corresponding equations for Model I, there are fewer degrees of freedom. However, the difference is minor; and the critical t values are virtually the same.

67. Keran and Babb made use of this idea in a similar study. See Keran and Babb, *Federal Reserve Actions*, p. 14. These authors suggest that the interested reader consult Arthur S. Goldberger, *Econometric Theory* (New York: John Wiley and Sons, Inc., 1964), pp. 197-198. The partial correlation coefficient could be used as an alternative, and parametric tests of equality used to determine whether or not differences in sample coefficients are statistically significant. Given the strong assumptions needed for such tests, however, I have chosen to base my conclusions on a ranking of the coefficients rather than on formal tests.

68. Once again, it is emphasized, however, that this conclusion (and the ones that follow) is based on the reduced form coefficients which include more than the weights of the disutility function. Hence, the conclusion that the primary goal was the stabilization of output does not *necessarily* follow from the apparent importance of fluctuations in O_t in explaining the fluctuations in $\Delta GS'_t$.

69. The beta coefficient of Δar_t is .80. Once again the effect of this variable seems to pale the significance of the other variables in the equation.

70. The beta coefficient of Δdr_t in the equation for Δar_t is .67.

71. The rates used were the rates at the New York Federal Reserve Bank.

72. See, for example, Friedman and Schwartz, *Monetary History*, pp. 266-268. Their discussion of the dispute over control by direct action is also relevant. (Ibid., pp. 254-266.)

73. The development of Model II does, however, allow for this possibility. See above.

74. The relevant simple correlation coefficients are shown below:

	Simple Correlation Coefficients Between		
Period	O_t & ERS_t	O_t & $\Delta GS'_t$	ERS_t & $\Delta GS'_t$
1924-1931	.54	-.23	-.18
1924-1927	.80	-.46	-.48

This multicollinearity is the other side of a coin previously examined. It was noted before that the exclusion of variables that are correlated with the included variables can bias the results. Unfortunately, the other side of the coin is that the *inclusion* of these correlated variables can make the results unreliable because of multicollinearity.

75. One further point regarding the bi-period analysis of Model II seems worth making. The coefficient of $\dot{SP}_t$ in the regression for 1924-1927 is not significant. It *is* significant in all the other regressions that cover or include later years. This suggests that stock

market speculation was not important in open market policy prior to 1928. This would seem to justify the treatment of the variable XSS, i.e., taking its value to be zero prior to November, 1927.

76. The beta coefficients for the variables in equation (3) are .81 for Δar_t, .16 for XSS_t and -.14 for XDA_t.

77. Burgess, *Federal Reserve Policy and Benjamin Strong*, p. 208. It might also be noted that Hardy considers the desire to establish an acceptance market in the United States to have been one of the minor goals of the Fed in the period under examination. (Hardy, *Credit Policies*, pp. 243-263.) Burgess reflects this sentiment when he stresses the desirability of having an acceptance market. (Burgess, *Federal Reserve Policy and Benjamin Strong*, pp. 146-148.) He maintains that, "The bill market could not exist without the Federal Reserve Banks . . ." (Ibid., p. 140). The reason that this is so is that the Federal Reserve Banks provided a place where the dealers in acceptances could always obtain funds during a "temporary period of stringency." (Ibid., p. 141.) It could also be added, however, that if the Reserve Banks were to serve this purpose their buying rate on acceptances must be close to the market rate. This, then, is probably the reason why the buying rate in acceptances closely followed the open market rate on acceptances.

78. I must thank Professor Fred M. Westfield for raising this question and thus forcing me to consider it explicitly.

79. See, for example, the alternative policies suggested by Friedman and Schwartz, *Monetary History*, pp. 391-407.

80. See, for example, Wood, *Federal Reserve Behavior*, pp. 149-156; and Bonomo and Schatta, *Spectral Analysis*, pp. 58-60.

81. The average daily holdings of acceptances by Federal Reserve Banks fell from around three or four hundred million dollars in the late 1920's to only five million dollars in 1935. See *Banking and Monetary Statistics*, pp. 370-371.

82. In addition, exploratory regressions indicated that this was, indeed, the case. Most of the variation in ΔA could be explained by the variation in other sources and uses of reserve funds, *including* purchases and sales of government securities. This means that open market operations could achieve only limited success in forcing member banks into debt.

CHAPTER FOUR

Summary

This study was undertaken to test alternative explanations of Federal Reserve behavior in the period 1923-1931 provided by a number of authors. In particular, it was desired to identify the determinants of Federal Reserve open market policy and its rate policy (discount and acceptance rates) in order to clarify the reasons for the failure of the System to undertake large purchases of government securities after the downturn of 1929. The study has been successful in achieving its goals, although that success has not been complete.

It was argued in the beginning that what was needed was an empirical test of Federal Reserve behavior based on its actual responses rather than statements of Fed officials. This study has provided that test through a regression analysis based on two similar models of Federal Reserve behavior derived from the policy statements of Reserve officials and from the studies of other scholars of the period. The alternative explanations offered by these scholars, which were based primarily on the official and private records of the System and its personnel, were given explicit formulation and subjected to statistical tests.

While the statistical tests are essential to an adequate understanding and interpretation of Reserve behavior, in a variety of instances their inadequacies have been apparent. What is really necessary is a blend of statistical evidence with the official and private records. In this way each type of evidence is subjected to the check of the other. Where the two different kinds of evidence conflict, it falls to the researcher to decide which evidence is more reliable as a basis for the conclusions drawn.[1]

This thesis has provided a mixture of evidence from both fields by emphasizing the statistical where others have emphasized the verbal. By drawing upon both, perhaps the conclusions reached in Chapter Three have served to clarify the determinants of Federal Reserve behavior and the reasons for the failure of the System to adequately respond to the beginnings of the Great Depression.

The models from which the regression analysis proceeded were based on the assumption that System officials acted as though they were minimizing a disutility function subject to the constraints imposed by their view of the workings of the economy. The two models differed in the degree of complexity of the disutility functions. The principal ingredient in both models of the economy (which imposed the constraints on Federal Reserve behavior) was the embodiment of the Riefler-Burgess doctrine in the sub-model of the market for credit.

The results of the regression analysis, when combined with the evidence offered by other students of the topic, provide a reasonably complete picture of the behavior of the Federal Reserve System and its officials.

From 1924 through 1927, it seems fairly clear that the Federal Reserve System was attempting to achieve *both* domestic stability and a return to the international gold standard. Fortunately, these goals were compatible during most of the period. The System could work toward the international goal by easing credit at home during two recessions which called for the same policy.

It would appear, however, that there is no basis for the contention that System officials were *primarily* interested in achieving the international goal if that meant sacrificing the domestic goals (in this period or later). It is also fairly clear that the countercyclical policy of the Fed was effected primarily through open market operations while the tools used for achieving the international goals were changes in the discount and acceptance rates as well as the direct extension of credit to foreign governments and support operations in foreign exchange.

From the end of 1927 until the stock market crash of October, 1929, the System attempted to stem the rising tide of speculation in stocks by restrictive open market and discount policies. The high level of output certainly provided no hinderance to such a policy, but the conclusion by Clarke that the policy damaged the international situation seems inescapable. Hence, the international goals seem to have been, at least temporarily, subordinated to the goal of ending stock market speculation.

After the crash, both open market and rate policies turned expansionary, at least for a while. It would have to be concluded, based on the regression results, that the initial response was to both the decline in output and the stock market crash. This is so because the negative relation between open market purchases and sales and stock market speculation indicates support for a falling market as well as restriction of a rising market.[2]

The Fed did not continue making large purchases into 1930 in part because of a fear of stimulating the stock market (which was showing signs of revival), in part because of an apparent stabilization of output, and in part because interest rates were already low and were continuing to fall. Later in the year and in 1931, System officials were apparently also divided over the efficacy of additional purchases. This, on top of unprecedently low rates, is probably a principal reason for inaction.

In the second half of 1931, member bank reserves fell for the first time during the depression (or any other recession during the period under examination). This was a result of the outflow of gold after Britain's departure from the gold standard and the subsequent worsening of the banking panic, which increased currency in circulation precipitously, and of the failure of Federal Reserve credit to expand to make up for this loss. While this has not been the question to which this thesis was addressed, it would appear that Friedman and Schwartz are correct in their conclusion that the greatest failure of the Fed was its failure to respond to the liquidity crisis.

With respect to the question of consistency of Federal Reserve behavior in its open market operations, the regression analysis provided no evidence of a change in its behavior before and after 1929. The behavior appears to have been consistent, with two possible exceptions. One of these is the possibly decreased importance of the international goal after 1927; the other is the possibility that Federal Reserve officials over-reacted to the low rates of 1930-1931 in the sense that purchases were restricted by these low rates more than would have been expected based on the earlier period.

While the evidence uncovered on these questions has not always been unambiguous, it should nevertheless be useful in solving the problem of what went wrong with monetary policy after 1929.

NOTES

1. Professor Anthony Tang has correctly pointed out that the conflict could be due to an incorrect specification of the disutility function. In particular, he suggests the use of a disutility function in which a single target enters but which is subject to side-order constraints involving inequalities such as "the unemployment rate must be less than or equal to six percent." This suggestion contains some interesting implications.

However, it was not possible to test all of the conceivable alternatives; and I suspect that in the end the investigator will still be forced to make a decision between conflicting results. The particular disutility function must, in my opinion, reflect the policy statements of the System officials as accurately as possible. But the exact formulation will likely differ from one researcher to another.

2. It is perhaps true that the initial response was more of a response to the stock market than to output. This is Friedman and Schwartz's conclusion (Friedman and Schwartz, *Monetary History*, pp. 339, 363-367).

Appendices

APPENDIX A

Data

Table A.I contains a list of the data used in the regression analysis and spectral analysis employed in this study. The sources of the data are cited in the notes to Table A.I.

The derivation of the dependent variable for open market purchases and sales (ΔGS') is illustrated in Table A.II. The explanation of its derivation given in Chapter Three needs no additional elaboration. However, the derivation of the variable to which the Fed is assumed to have responded in its "defensive" operations (ΔRR') does need further explanation.

As stated in Chapter Three, there are no monthly data available for excess or required reserves prior to 1929. There are data available, however, for call dates. Using these data (for excess reserves and total deposits of member banks), the effective required reserve ratio (ERR) was obtained. The relevant data and the results are given in Table A.III.

Table A.I shows the effective reserve ratio and the ratio of net demand deposits to time deposits (NDD/TD) for the years 1923-1928. There appears to be a strong positive relation between these two variables, and both declined over the years 1923-1928. The decline in ERR is, of course, to be expected because of the decline in the ratio of demand to time deposits. The latter decline is apparently the result of a desire by member banks to shift demand deposits to time deposits to take advantage of the lower reserve requirement for time deposits.[1]

Further calculations showed that there was a factor working to increase the effective required reserve ratio during these years (1923-1928). The estimated effective reserve ratio on demand deposits only (ERRDD) increased over these years.[2] (See Table A.IV.)

It was decided that the best means of capturing both of these effects in a regression analysis was to regress the effective reserve ratio on the ratio of net demand deposits to time deposits *and* a time trend to represent the increasing effective reserve requirements for demand deposits.[3] Since the latter requirements rose over time, the time trend should exhibit a positive effect.

Two regressions were run on the data for call dates—one linear and one log-linear. All of the coefficients had the expected signs in both of these regressions, and both regressions fit the data very well. It was impossible to choose the "better" fit, and the log-linear regression was arbitrarily chosen. This regression is:

$$\text{Log}(ERR_t) = \underset{(-158.3)}{-1.196} + \underset{(12.63)}{.2382}\,(NDD/TD) + \underset{(3.71)}{.0085}\log(t) \qquad \bar{R}^2 = .95 \quad DW = 1.54$$

The next step was to estimate the monthly effective required reserve ratio using the above regression results and monthly data for net demand deposits and time deposits for member banks. These data and the estimated effective reserve requirements are listed in Table A.V. Finally, by applying the estimated effective reserve ratio to the total deposits of member banks, estimates of required reserves were obtained. These estimates, and the estimates of excess reserves obtained by subtracting the estimated required reserves from total reserves, are also given in Table A.V.

Based on the first differences of the estimates of required reserves listed in Table A.V., the variable $\Delta RR'$ was obtained for the years 1924-1928. This variable is listed in Table A.I.

TABLE A.I.
DATA

Year	Month	ΔGS'	Δdr	Δar	XSS	$S\dot{P}$	O	$\dot{P}$	r_L	BT
1923	Jan.	n.a.	0.00	0.00	0.00	0.0	99	0.9	2.28	-7
	Feb.	n.a.	0.50	0.00	0.00	2.9	100	1.1	2.49	25
	Mar.	n.a.	0.00	0.00	0.00	2.2	103	1.2	2.28	-27
	Apr.	n.a.	0.00	0.13	0.00	-0.9	106	0.1	2.10	-18
	May	n.a.	0.00	0.00	0.00	-3.4	106	-1.0	2.03	-22
	June	n.a.	0.00	0.00	0.00	-3.9	106	-1.5	2.10	26
	July	n.a.	0.00	0.00	0.00	-3.6	104	-1.8	3.23	46
	Aug.	n.a.	0.00	0.00	0.00	-1.2	103	-1.1	3.18	58
	Sept.	n.a.	0.00	0.00	0.00	0.0	100	0.6	3.17	110
	Oct.	n.a.	0.00	0.00	0.00	-0.6	99	0.3	3.17	39
	Nov.	n.a.	0.00	0.00	0.00	1.4	98	-0.3	3.30	49
	Dec.	n.a.	0.00	0.00	0.00	2.4	97	-0.5	3.31	96
1924	Jan.	28	0.00	0.00	0.00	3.2	100	0.6	3.29	85
	Feb.	29	0.00	0.00	0.00	1.6	102	0.4	3.54	59
	Mar.	87	0.00	0.00	0.00	-0.5	100	-0.4	3.20	42
	Apr.	51	0.00	-0.13	0.00	-1.8	95	-1.0	3.07	43
	May	52	-0.50	-0.75	0.00	-1.1	89	-1.3	3.05	67
	June	94	-0.50	-1.00	0.00	0.6	85	-1.1	3.03	59
	July	49	0.00	0.00	0.00	3.1	84	-0.0	3.59	25
	Aug.	73	-0.50	0.00	0.00	3.5	89	0.9	3.79	101
	Sept.	37	0.00	0.00	0.00	1.0	94	0.5	3.74	120
	Oct.	6	0.00	0.00	0.00	-0.5	95	0.8	3.72	143
	Nov.	5	0.00	0.25	0.00	2.6	97	0.8	3.72	123
	Dec.	-58	0.00	0.50	0.00	4.4	101	1.8	3.73	69

Table A.I.
DATA *(Continued)*

Year	Month	ΔGS'	Δdr	Δar	XSS	$S\dot{P}$	O	$\dot{P}$	r_L	BT
1925	Jan.	-67	0.00	0.00	0.00	4.6	105	1.6	3.80	87
	Feb.	-80	0.50	0.13	0.00	2.4	104	1.3	3.83	64
	Mar.	-25	0.00	0.00	0.00	-0.6	103	0.6	4.48	91
	Apr.	-15	0.00	0.00	0.00	-1.1	102	-1.0	4.30	75
	May	-2	0.00	0.00	0.00	1.1	102	-0.7	4.59	82
	June	-5	0.00	0.12	0.00	1.7	102	0.3	4.44	41
	July	-20	0.00	0.00	0.00	2.5	103	1.0	4.35	44
	Aug.	2	0.00	0.13	0.00	1.8	103	0.3	3.94	62
	Sept.	-3	0.00	0.00	0.00	2.1	101	-0.2	3.68	40
	Oct.	1	0.00	0.00	0.00	2.7	104	-0.0	3.57	43
	Nov.	0	0.00	0.00	0.00	3.1	107	0.4	3.92	13
	Dec.	15	0.00	0.00	0.00	2.3	109	-0.3	4.67	33
1926	Jan.	35	0.50	0.25	0.00	1.7	106	-0.2	4.76	-32
	Feb.	-35	0.00	0.00	0.00	0.6	105	-0.8	4.31	-12
	Mar.	-5	0.00	0.00	0.00	-3.1	106	-1.1	4.37	-39
	Apr.	44	-0.50	-0.13	0.00	-3.4	107	-0.7	4.33	14
	May	23	0.00	-0.25	0.00	-1.5	106	-0.1	4.37	73
	June	-5	0.00	0.00	0.00	2.1	108	-0.0	4.27	46
	July	-16	0.00	0.00	0.00	2.9	108	-0.5	4.26	63
	Aug.	-20	0.50	0.50	0.00	3.0	110	-0.5	4.45	71
	Sept.	-51	0.00	0.00	0.00	2.0	111	0.1	4.54	73
	Oct.	-2	0.00	0.00	0.00	-0.6	111	-0.0	4.69	11
	Nov.	-1	0.00	0.00	0.00	0.3	110	-0.5	4.57	44
	Dec.	9	0.00	0.00	0.00	1.3	107	-0.6	4.53	68

TABLE A.I.
DATA *(Continued)*

Year	Month	$\Delta GS'$	Δdr	Δar	XSS	$S\dot{P}$	O	$\dot{P}$	r_L	BT
1927	Jan.	-5	0.00	0.00	0.00	0.9	107	-1.1	4.17	50
	Feb.	3	0.00	0.00	0.00	1.6	108	-0.9	4.19	89
	Mar.	7	0.00	0.00	0.00	1.2	110	-1.0	4.33	54
	Apr.	6	0.00	0.00	0.00	1.6	108	-0.7	4.04	63
	May	-34	0.00	0.00	0.00	2.2	109	-0.2	3.88	88
	June	106	0.00	0.00	0.00	1.6	107	-0.1	4.34	49
	July	-14	0.00	-0.25	0.00	1.5	106	0.1	4.33	53
	Aug.	60	-0.50	-0.25	0.00	2.9	106	0.5	4.33	27
	Sept.	44	0.00	0.00	0.00	4.0	104	0.9	4.32	53
	Oct.	18	0.00	0.00	0.00	1.4	102	0.6	4.32	59
	Nov.	32	0.00	0.00	0.05	1.7	101	0.0	4.33	57
	Dec.	13	0.00	0.00	0.08	2.0	102	0.0	4.31	43
1928	Jan.	-60	0.00	0.13	0.07	1.6	107	-0.0	4.19	61
	Feb.	-83	0.50	0.12	-0.01	-0.2	109	-0.3	4.18	46
	Mar.	-4	0.00	0.13	0.17	2.1	108	-0.3	4.12	63
	Apr.	-56	0.00	0.12	0.33	4.3	108	0.4	4.02	40
	May	-94	0.50	0.25	0.49	4.6	108	0.8	3.97	112
	June	-40	0.00	0.00	0.37	-0.5	108	-0.0	3.82	125
	July	-7	0.50	0.50	0.40	-1.1	109	0.3	3.99	98
	Aug.	1	0.00	0.00	0.58	0.7	110	0.2	4.27	55
	Sept.	13	0.00	0.00	0.79	3.9	113	0.7	4.23	73
	Oct.	9	0.00	0.00	0.85	2.9	115	-0.7	4.35	109
	Nov.	-19	0.00	0.00	1.05	5.5	117	-0.9	4.38	148
	Dec.	-2	0.00	0.00	0.99	2.4	118	-0.5	4.37	97

TABLE A.I.
DATA *(Continued)*

Year	Month	ΔGS'	Δdr	Δar	XSS	$S\dot{P}$	O	$\dot{P}$	r_L	BT
1929	Jan.	1	0.00	0.50	1.24	5.7	119	-0.0	4.32	105
	Feb.	-20	0.00	0.13	1.27	2.7	118	-0.2	5.05	105
	Mar.	-17	0.00	0.37	1.38	2.1	118	0.2	5.33	129
	Apr.	-11	0.00	0.00	1.34	-0.2	121	-0.2	5.21	40
	May	-15	0.00	0.00	1.32	0.1	122	-0.5	5.21	26
	June	-3	0.00	0.00	1.35	0.8	125	-0.0	5.32	93
	July	-9	0.00	-0.25	1.57	5.5	124	0.8	5.38	88
	Aug.	1	1.00	-0.12	1.73	5.6	121	0.3	5.47	33
	Sept.	-1	0.00	0.00	1.84	4.5	121	0.0	5.59	55
	Oct.	15	0.00	-0.13	1.40	-4.2	118	-0.6	6.13	57
	Nov.	166	-1.50	-1.00	0.16	-16.8	110	-1.2	5.35	46
	Dec.	106	0.00	0.00	0.16	-7.6	103	-0.7	4.76	82
1930	Jan.	65	0.00	0.00	0.06	-2.1	106	-0.7	4.07	88
	Feb.	-1	-0.50	-0.25	0.51	4.0	107	-0.9	3.82	93
	Mar.	33	-0.50	-0.75	0.56	4.3	103	-1.2	2.78	87
	Apr.	17	0.00	0.00	0.76	4.8	104	-0.6	2.48	43
	May	1	-0.50	-0.50	-0.52	-1.2	102	-1.0	2.16	69
	June	37	-0.50	-0.50	0.03	-6.8	98	-1.7	2.31	85
	July	13	0.00	-0.25	0.05	-5.1	93	-2.4	2.37	72
	Aug.	20	0.00	0.00	0.01	-2.7	90	-1.1	2.21	99
	Sept.	-8	0.00	0.00	0.08	-0.1	90	-0.3	2.07	64
	Oct.	12	0.00	0.00	0.00	-8.0	88	-0.9	2.09	30
	Nov.	-3	0.00	0.00	0.00	-8.8	86	-1.6	2.18	48
	Dec.	28	-0.50	0.00	0.00	-8.0	84	-2.0	2.30	44

TABLE A.I.
DATA *(Continued)*

Year	Month	ΔGS'	Δdr	Δar	XSS	$S\dot{P}$	O	$\dot{P}$	r_L	BT
1931	Jan.	13	0.00	-0.12	0.00	-1.4	83	-1.9	2.25	59
	Feb.	-37	0.00	0.00	0.00	3.6	86	-1.8	2.56	66
	Mar.	-7	0.00	0.00	0.00	3.1	87	-1.3	2.60	39
	Apr.	3	0.00	-0.25	0.00	-4.4	88	-1.4	2.58	42
	May	0	-0.50	-0.38	0.00	-8.5	87	-1.8	2.24	46
	June	9	0.00	0.00	0.00	-6.0	83	-1.6	2.09	39
	July	66	0.00	0.00	0.00	-0.4	82	-0.8	2.58	22
	Aug.	38	0.00	0.00	0.00	-1.0	78	-0.1	4.28	7
	Sept.	15	0.00	0.25	0.00	-8.5	76	-0.6	4.74	-4
	Oct.	5	2.00	1.88	0.00	-12.9	73	-1.0	5.68	6
	Nov.	-5	0.00	0.00	0.00	-4.6	73	-0.6	5.75	19
	Dec.	11	0.00	0.00	0.00	-12.4	74	-1.5	5.85	15

Year	Month	ΔG	G	ERS	ΔRR'	ΔN	IDRP	r	IMC
1923	Jan.	25	3655	4.65	n.a.	n.a.	0.03	4.50	0.44
	Feb.	18	3673	4.69	n.a.	n.a.	1.10	4.63	0.65
	Mar.	6	3679	4.69	n.a.	n.a.	0.03	5.13	0.92
	Apr.	9	3688	4.65	n.a.	n.a.	0.34	5.38	1.02
	May	18	3706	4.62	n.a.	-2	0.03	5.00	1.15
	June	47	3753	4.61	n.a.	131	0.03	5.00	1.23
	July	21	3774	4.58	n.a.	10	0.03	5.13	1.43
	Aug.	36	3810	4.56	n.a.	31	0.03	5.13	1.38
	Sept.	26	3836	4.54	n.a.	56	0.03	5.38	1.45
	Oct.	32	3868	4.52	n.a.	-14	0.03	5.38	1.51
	Nov.	27	3895	4.38	n.a.	-48	0.03	5.13	1.36
	Dec.	44	3939	4.36	n.a.	63	0.03	5.00	1.30

TABLE A.I.
DATA *(Continued)*

Year	Month	ΔG	G	ERS	ΔRR'	ΔN	IDRP	r	IMC
1924	Jan.	40	3979	4.25	-321	-360	0.03	4.88	0.88
	Feb.	36	4015	4.30	34	-7	0.03	4.88	0.75
	Mar.	38	4053	4.29	62	-36	0.03	4.88	0.67
	Apr.	43	4096	4.35	3	-16	-0.28	4.63	0.68
	May	50	4146	4.36	23	-36	-2.83	4.50	-0.03
	June	38	4184	4.32	-38	-133	-3.43	4.13	-0.78
	July	32	4216	4.37	-13	-63	0.03	3.50	-1.33
	Aug.	13	4229	4.49	67	2	-1.04	3.25	-1.66
	Sept.	-1	4228	4.46	30	-3	0.03	3.13	-1.75
	Oct.	-9	4219	4.48	-25	-34	0.03	3.13	-1.80
	Nov.	11	4230	4.61	32	35	0.63	3.25	-1.75
	Dec.	-10	4220	4.69	62	107	1.23	3.63	-1.37
1925	Jan.	-39	4181	4.78	-218	-105	0.03	3.63	-1.31
	Feb.	-76	4105	4.77	101	164	1.41	3.63	-1.14
	Mar.	-52	4053	4.77	-26	-6	0.03	4.00	-0.66
	Apr.	0	4053	4.79	22	17	0.03	4.00	-0.63
	May	13	4066	4.85	13	13	0.03	3.88	-0.64
	June	7	4073	4.86	28	55	0.32	3.88	-0.53
	July	1	4074	4.86	-18	-18	0.03	3.88	-0.40
	Aug.	11	4085	4.85	119	119	0.34	4.00	-0.26
	Sept.	14	4099	4.84	51	56	0.03	4.25	-0.09
	Oct.	5	4104	4.84	-27	-29	0.03	4.38	-0.04
	Nov.	16	4120	4.84	39	39	0.03	4.38	-0.09
	Dec.	-10	4110	4.85	171	148	0.03	4.38	0.11

TABLE A.I.
DATA *(Continued)*

Year	Month	ΔG	G	ERS	ΔRR'	ΔN	IDRP	r	IMC
1926	Jan.	10	4120	4.85	-292	-317	1.69	4.38	0.09
	Feb.	18	4138	4.86	57	99	0.03	4.25	0.20
	Mar.	19	4157	4.86	18	40	0.03	4.38	0.27
	Apr.	4	4161	4.86	-26	-114	-1.35	4.38	0.14
	May	-14	4147	4.86	13	9	-0.57	4.00	-0.24
	June	4	4151	4.86	-43	-25	0.03	4.00	-0.42
	July	22	4173	4.86	57	62	0.03	4.00	-0.27
	Aug.	7	4180	4.85	-3	46	2.29	4.38	-0.01
	Sept.	1	4181	4.85	57	81	0.03	4.63	0.50
	Oct.	4	4185	4.85	-6	-8	0.03	4.63	0.55
	Nov.	5	4190	4.84	7	6	0.03	4.50	0.45
	Dec.	4	4194	4.85	95	89	0.03	4.50	0.56
1927	Jan.	46	4240	4.85	-348	-346	0.03	4.25	0.16
	Feb.	49	4289	4.85	66	63	0.03	4.13	-0.03
	Mar.	19	4308	4.85	-33	-46	0.03	4.13	0.04
	Apr.	6	4314	4.85	13	17	0.03	4.13	0.09
	May	50	5364	4.85	-7	5	0.03	4.13	0.14
	June	-45	4319	4.85	42	-21	0.03	4.25	0.05
	July	-31	4288	4.85	4	-11	-0.57	4.25	0.10
	Aug.	10	4298	4.85	49	-13	-1.64	4.00	-0.47
	Sept.	-1	4297	4.86	51	9	0.03	4.00	-0.55
	Oct.	-18	4279	4.87	11	-13	0.03	4.00	-0.54
	Nov.	-76	4203	4.87	90	68	0.03	4.00	-0.56
	Dec.	-74	4129	4.88	12	-1	0.03	4.00	-0.32

TABLE A.I.
DATA *(Continued)*

Year	Month	ΔG	G	ERS	ΔRR'	ΔN	IDRP	r	IMC
1928	Jan.	-39	4090	4.87	-82	-60	0.34	4.00	-0.40
	Feb.	-4	4086	4.87	-79	43	1.38	4.00	0.00
	Mar.	-38	4048	4.88	55	55	0.34	4.13	0.09
	Apr.	-48	4000	4.88	71	101	0.32	4.38	0.51
	May	-80	3920	4.88	54	160	1.69	4.50	1.14
	June	-88	3832	4.88	237	288	0.03	4.75	1.75
	July	-6	3826	4.86	24	34	2.29	5.13	2.16
	Aug.	5	3831	4.85	14	19	0.03	5.38	2.43
	Sept.	7	3838	4.85	-19	-34	0.03	5.63	2.43
	Oct.	8	3846	4.85	-31	-30	0.03	5.50	2.24
	Nov.	18	3864	4.84	-41	-27	0.03	5.38	2.08
	Dec.	-9	3855	4.85	13	7	0.03	5.38	2.32
1929	Jan.	-27	3828	4.85	-161	-159	1.23	5.38	2.13
	Feb.	28	3856	4.85	17	37	0.34	5.50	2.37
	Mar.	23	3879	4.85	70	87	0.91	5.88	2.65
	Apr.	60	3939	4.85	33	44	0.03	6.00	2.87
	May	66	4005	4.85	-62	-47	0.03	6.00	2.76
	June	19	4024	4.84	6	9	0.03	6.00	2.80
	July	24	4048	4.85	109	118	-0.57	6.00	2.98
	Aug.	16	4064	4.84	-46	-47	1.88	6.13	2.91
	Sept.	17	4081	4.84	-73	-72	0.03	6.25	3.19
	Oct.	13	4094	4.87	-77	-92	-0.28	6.25	2.99
	Nov.	-7	4087	4.87	211	45	-5.56	5.75	2.00
	Dec.	-50	4037	4.88	-27	-133	0.03	5.00	1.29

TABLE A.I.
DATA *(Continued)*

Year	Month	ΔG	G	ERS	ΔRR'	ΔN	IDRP	r	IMC
1930	Jan.	-41	3996	4.86	-233	-298	0.03	4.88	0.65
	Feb.	34	4030	4.86	-133	-132	-1.64	4.75	0.09
	Mar.	77	4107	4.86	-74	-107	-2.83	4.25	-0.66
	Apr.	49	4156	4.86	-12	-29	0.03	3.88	-1.09
	May	62	4218	4.86	14	13	-2.23	3.75	-1.57
	June	23	4241	4.85	32	-5	-2.23	3.50	-1.87
	July	4	4245	4.86	-32	-45	-0.57	3.25	-2.30
	Aug.	-36	4209	4.87	30	10	0.03	3.00	-2.43
	Sept.	7	4216	4.86	-40	-32	0.03	3.00	-2.49
	Oct.	17	4233	4.85	19	7	0.03	3.00	-2.47
	Nov.	33	4266	4.85	29	32	0.03	2.88	-2.42
	Dec.	30	4296	4.85	124	96	-1.04	2.88	-2.24
1931	Jan.	39	4335	4.85	-104	-117	-0.26	2.88	-2.71
	Feb.	34	4369	4.85	-26	11	0.03	2.63	-2.80
	Mar.	26	4395	4.85	-56	-49	0.03	2.50	-2.89
	Apr.	29	4424	4.86	-8	-11	-0.57	2.38	-3.00
	May	56	4480	4.86	-3	-3	-1.95	2.25	-3.23
	June	98	4578	4.86	-26	-35	0.03	2.00	-3.51
	July	93	4671	4.85	50	-16	0.03	2.00	-3.56
	Aug.	17	4688	4.85	115	77	0.03	2.00	-3.44
	Sept.	-27	4661	4.53	55	40	0.63	2.00	-3.29
	Oct.	-501	4160	3.88	328	323	8.80	3.13	-1.12
	Nov.	-84	4076	3.72	148	153	0.03	4.00	-0.03
	Dec.	87	4163	3.37	87	76	0.03	3.88	0.14

TABLE A.I.
DATA *(Continued)*

Year	Month	B	dr	ar	ΔGS	ΔA	ΔM	ΔRR	ΔR	ΔB
1923	Jan.	547	4.00	4.00	41	-41	-148	18	78	-113
	Feb.	608	4.13	4.00	-65	-28	-7	-10	-17	61
	Mar.	628	4.50	4.00	-40	44	41	-17	-28	20
	Apr.	658	4.50	4.07	-87	38	18	24	-4	30
	May	705	4.50	4.13	-36	-1	33	10	5	47
	June	741	4.50	4.13	-40	-47	15	12	-7	36
	July	834	4.50	4.13	-56	-38	33	13	0	93
	Aug.	809	4.50	4.13	-7	-11	21	-4	-32	-25
	Sept.	845	4.50	4.13	12	-1	68	8	13	36
	Oct.	873	4.50	4.13	-11	11	40	-4	16	28
	Nov.	799	4.50	4.13	-8	80	12	-2	11	-74
	Dec.	771	4.50	4.13	23	59	118	27	7	-28
1924	Jan.	574	4.50	4.13	12	-24	-224	-26	29	-197
	Feb.	514	4.50	4.13	17	-27	-15	0	-19	-60
	Mar.	476	4.50	4.13	109	-45	38	-3	23	-38
	Apr.	489	4.50	4.10	30	-58	16	-22	-10	13
	May	433	4.00	3.60	50	-90	-20	43	17	-56
	June	370	3.75	2.75	92	-30	-36	6	79	-63
	July	315	3.50	2.25	51	-6	-20	3	45	-55
	Aug.	268	3.13	2.25	72	-14	-10	-8	26	-47
	Sept.	262	3.00	2.25	36	62	53	10	48	-6
	Oct.	240	3.00	2.25	10	88	38	-8	21	-22
	Nov.	228	3.00	2.38	3	88	79	12	23	-12
	Dec.	307	3.00	2.75	-34	90	118	11	18	79

TABLE A.I.
DATA *(Continued)*

Year	Month	B	dr	ar	ΔGS	ΔA	ΔM	ΔRR	ΔR	ΔB
1925	Jan.	275	3.00	3.00	-90	-29	-225	-23	12	-32
	Feb.	351	3.00	3.00	-80	-16	-58	3	-35	76
	Mar.	400	3.50	3.13	-8	-15	9	13	-22	49
	Apr.	413	3.50	3.13	-21	-11	-11	-6	-14	13
	May	408	3.50	3.13	6	-8	-12	-9	9	-5
	June	448	3.50	3.18	-16	-16	-1	-7	9	40
	July	491	3.50	3.25	-7	-32	4	18	19	43
	Aug.	556	3.50	3.25	-9	-26	23	-27	-9	65
	Sept.	602	3.50	3.38	6	21	91	14	10	46
	Oct.	626	3.50	3.38	-7	72	37	-15	42	24
	Nov.	602	3.50	3.38	4	54	15	-17	18	-24
	Dec.	696	3.50	3.38	27	17	159	29	-2	94
1926	Jan.	527	3.88	3.57	9	-45	-228	-16	17	-169
	Feb.	533	4.00	3.63	-33	-19	-37	-37	-28	6
	Mar.	565	4.00	3.63	1	-37	10	-15	-10	32
	Apr.	546	3.88	3.60	35	-34	18	17	-15	-19
	May	519	3.50	3.44	27	-2	-11	21	16	-27
	June	480	3.50	3.25	10	11	10	31	7	-39
	July	553	3.50	3.25	-28	-13	35	-13	6	73
	Aug.	555	3.75	3.44	-27	15	-4	-12	-11	2
	Sept.	640	4.00	3.75	-37	20	57	-2	10	85
	Oct.	663	4.00	3.75	-10	30	32	-7	8	23
	Nov.	615	4.00	3.75	-4	53	4	-7	-5	-48
	Dec.	668	4.00	3.75	20	37	126	16	4	53

TABLE A.I.
DATA *(Continued)*

Year	Month	B	dr	ar	ΔGS	ΔA	ΔM	ΔRR	ΔR	ΔB
1927	Jan.	481	4.00	3.75	-12	-42	-228	-8	25	-187
	Feb.	393	4.00	3.75	-3	-39	-60	-10	-31	-88
	Mar.	425	4.00	3.75	38	-51	13	3	28	32
	Apr.	447	4.00	3.75	-4	-5	23	12	8	22
	May	473	4.00	3.75	-50	-15	-19	-16	14	26
	June	429	4.00	3.75	107	-28	-29	20	39	-44
	July	454	4.00	3.75	-17	-15	20	46	-12	25
	Aug.	409	3.63	3.30	58	-17	-2	-14	-6	-45
	Sept.	422	3.50	3.25	62	43	68	-32	17	13
	Oct.	424	3.50	3.25	5	66	14	-15	26	2
	Nov.	415	3.50	3.25	73	54	5	10	47	-9
	Dec.	529	3.50	3.25	27	42	112	29	26	114
1928	Jan.	465	3.50	3.35	-94	-5	-263	-34	27	-64
	Feb.	471	4.00	3.50	-106	-13	-76	-17	-58	6
	Mar.	513	4.00	3.50	9	-17	1	2	-3	42
	Apr.	661	4.00	3.69	-64	15	20	0	31	148
	May	836	4.25	3.88	-94	-9	-8	-8	-8	175
	June	1019	4.50	4.00	-25	-105	14	16	-33	183
	July	1090	4.75	4.19	-19	-59	10	-8	-31	71
	Aug.	1061	5.00	4.50	-3	-7	-3	-19	-50	-29
	Sept.	1064	5.00	4.50	30	48	61	13	40	3
	Oct.	975	5.00	4.50	-3	142	32	-8	18	-89
	Nov.	897	5.00	4.50	1	103	24	0	20	-78
	Dec.	1013	5.00	4.50	25	12	148	19	15	116

TABLE A.I.
DATA *(Continued)*

Year	Month	B	dr	ar	ΔGS	ΔA	ΔM	ΔRR	ΔR	ΔB
1929	Jan.	859	5.00	4.75	-34	-10	-260	-15	20	-154
	Feb.	889	5.00	5.07	-45	-88	-62	-17	-30	30
	Mar.	971	5.00	5.25	13	-120	23	5	-20	82
	Apr.	1010	5.00	5.50	-32	-109	-30	-17	-29	39
	May	960	5.00	5.50	-12	-11	5	0	-12	-50
	June	978	5.00	5.50	26	-46	3	4	18	18
	July	1096	5.00	5.37	-32	-24	77	11	20	118
	Aug.	1043	5.25	5.16	8	49	13	-19	-12	-53
	Sept.	969	6.00	5.13	10	105	34	-11	13	-74
	Oct.	885	6.00	5.10	-11	108	-1	24	51	-84
	Nov.	953	4.75	4.44	161	-41	35	-11	135	68
	Dec.	803	4.50	4.00	131	24	98	17	-126	-150
1930	Jan.	501	4.50	4.00	39	-6	-291	-27	-46	-302
	Feb.	378	4.13	3.88	-5	-29	-98	-19	-44	-123
	Mar.	274	3.75	3.35	60	-39	-22	9	25	-104
	Apr.	231	3.50	3.00	-10	20	-14	-10	20	-43
	May	247	3.00	2.63	-1	-84	-21	-8	6	16
	June	251	2.88	2.20	42	-41	-8	0	36	4
	July	226	2.50	1.94	12	13	-6	15	25	-25
	Aug.	214	2.50	1.75	16	-1	-7	1	-25	-12
	Sept.	189	2.50	1.75	-2	44	17	-2	5	-25
	Oct.	196	2.50	1.75	5	-12	8	1	10	7
	Nov.	221	2.50	1.75	-3	-1	27	-1	26	25
	Dec.	338	2.38	1.75	45	73	295	12	-18	117

TABLE A.I.
DATA *(Continued)*

Year	Month	B	dr	ar	ΔGS	ΔA	ΔM	ΔRR	ΔR	ΔB
1931	Jan.	253	2.00	1.66	3	-51	-128	-15	18	-85
	Feb.	216	2.00	1.63	-44	-104	-97	-10	-63	-37
	Mar.	176	2.00	1.63	1	21	-8	0	16	-40
	Apr.	155	2.00	1.50	-4	50	57	-7	-10	-21
	May	163	1.88	1.19	-1	-29	32	9	11	8
	June	190	1.50	1.00	11	-23	71	-25	17	27
	July	169	1.50	1.00	64	-42	86	-5	3	-21
	Aug.	223	1.50	1.00	38	56	111	-116	-62	54
	Sept.	282	1.50	1.05	24	124	186	-6	-12	59
	Oct.	614	2.75	2.30	-3	433	345	7	-77	332
	Nov.	695	3.50	3.13	-6	-132	40	43	-138	81
	Dec.	774	3.50	3.13	50	-220	93	48	-49	79

Note: n.a. — data unavailable.

Description and sources of data:

ΔGS' The first difference of the average daily stock of government securities held by the Federal Reserve System (Fed) exclusive of one- and two-day Treasury certificates and securities held under resale agreements, adjusted for Treasury-related sales. (Millions of dollars.) See text and Table A.II for derivation and sources.

Δdr The first difference of the discount rate at the Federal Reserve Bank of New York, computed from the rate prevailing on the last day of the previous and present months. *Banking and Monetary Statistics*, pp. 439-441.

TABLE A.I. *(Continued)*

Δar The first difference of the buying rate on 61-90 day prime bankers' acceptances at the Federal Reserve Bank of New York, computed from the rate prevailing on the last day of the previous and present months. Ibid., pp. 444-445.

XSS The proxy variable for stock market speculation, valued at zero for January, 1923, through October, 1927, and October, 1930, through December, 1931. For November, 1927, through September, 1931, the variable takes on the value of the difference between the yield on 60 bonds and the yield on 90 common stocks (both compiled by Standard Statistics Co.). U.S. Department of Commerce, *Annual Supplement to the Survey of Current Business, 1932* (Washington, D.C.: U.S. Government Printing Office, 1933), pp. 98-99, 104-105.

$S\dot{P}$ A weighted average of the percentage increase in the Standard Statistics Common stock prices index over the past three months with geometrically declining weights (4, 2, 1). Basic data on stock prices from U.S. Federal Reserve Board, *Seventeenth Annual Report* (Washington, D.C.: U.S. Government Printing Office, 1931), p. 214; and *Twenty-first Annual Report* (Washington, D.C.: U.S. Government Printing Office, 1935), p. 233.

O Index of total industrial production (1923-1925 = 100), seasonally adjusted, compiled by the Federal Reserve Board, U.S. Federal Reserve Board, *Twentieth Annual Report* (Washington, D.C.: U.S. Government Printing Office, 1934), pp. 236-241.

$\dot{P}$ A weighted average of the percentage increase in the Bureau of Labor Statistics wholesale price index over the past three months with geometrically declining weights (4, 2, 1). Basic data on wholesale prices from U.S. Bureau of the Census, *Historical Statistics of the United States, 1789-1945* (Washington, D.C.: U.S. Government Printing Office, 1949), p. 344.

TABLE A.I. *(Continued)*

r_L Average rate on three month bank bills in London. Data for the years 1924-1931 from *Banking and Monetary Statistics*, pp. 656-658. Data for 1923 derived by taking the simple arithmetic mean of the monthly averages of the highest and lowest daily rates from *Statistical Abstract for the United Kingdom (1913 and 1922-35)* (London: H.M. Stationary Office, 1937), p. 235.

BT Net exports in millions of dollars derived from export and import data (seasonally adjusted). *Historical Statistics, 1789-1945*, pp. 339-340.

ΔG The first difference of the average daily monetary gold stock of the United States in millions of dollars. *Banking and Monetary Statistics*, pp. 369-371.

G The average daily monetary gold stock of the United States in millions of dollars. Ibid.

ERS The exchange rate for sterling ($ per £). Ibid., p. 681.

ΔRR' The first difference of required reserves less the first difference of the sum of all sources other than borrowings and government securities plus the first difference in uses of funds other than reserves. (Millions of dollars.) See text and Table A.V. Data on sources and uses of reserve funds from ibid., pp 369-371.

ΔN The first difference of required reserves less the first difference of the sum of all sources other than borrowings plus the first difference in uses of funds and other than reserves. (Millions of dollars.) See text and Table A.V. Data on sources and uses of reserve funds from ibid.

TABLE A.I. *(Continued)*

IDRP The variable for the common change in the discount and acceptance rates taken to be an indicator of the change in Federal Reserve rate policy. This is the first principal component of the variation in Δdr and Δar. In particular, IDRP is equal to .707 times the standardized Δdr plus .707 times the standardized Δar. For sources of Δdr and Δar, see above.

r The average open market rate of interest on 4-6 month prime commercial paper in New York City. *Banking and Monetary Statistics,* pp. 450-451.

IMC The variable used to represent the state of the supply side of the market for short-term credit. This is the first principal component of the variation in B, dr, and ar. In particular, IMC is equal to .559 times the standardized B plus .585 times the standardized dr plus .587 times the standardized ar. For sources of B, dr, and ar, see below.

B Average daily holdings of bills discounted by the Fed in millions of dollars. *Banking and Monetary Statistics,* pp. 369-371.

dr The average discount rate at the Federal Reserve Bank of New York, computed by weighting the prevailing rate by the number of weeks in effect. Prevailing rate from ibid., pp. 439-441.

ar The average buying rate on 61-90 day prime banker's acceptances at the Federal Reserve Bank of New York, computed by weighting the prevailing rate by the number of weeks in effect. Prevailing rate from ibid., pp. 444-445.

ΔGS The first difference in the average daily holdings of government securities by the Fed, in millions of dollars. Ibid., pp. 369-371.

TABLE A.I. *(Continued)*

ΔA	The first difference in the average daily holdings of bankers' acceptances purchased (or "bills bought") by the Fed, in millions of dollars. Ibid.
ΔM	The first difference of average daily currency in circulation in millions of dollars. Ibid.
ΔRR	The first difference of the average daily sources of reserve funds other than Fed holdings of government securities, acceptances, and bills discounted, and the monetary gold stock, less uses other than reserves and currency in circulation. Alternatively, ΔRR is the first difference of the average daily "other" Reserve Bank credit outstanding plus Treasury currency outstanding, less Treasury cash holdings, Treasury and non-member deposits with the Reserve Banks, and "other" Federal Reserve accounts. (Millions of dollars.) Data on these components from ibid.
ΔR	The first difference of the average daily reserves of member banks in millions of dollars. Ibid.
ΔB	The first difference of the average daily holdings of bills discounted by the Fed, in millions of dollars. Ibid.

TABLE A.II

ILLUSTRATION OF DERIVATION OF ΔGS' BASED ON DATA FOR FEBRUARY AND MARCH, 1925
(Figures are in millions of dollars)

Average Daily Holdings of U.S. Securities	February 1-28 (a)	March 1-15 (b)	March 16-22* (c)	March 23-31 (d)	March 1-31 (e)
(1) In System Account	291	272	233	245	255
Outside of System Account					
(2) Under Resale Agreement	2	16	1	4	9
(3) One-day Treasury Certificates	0	0	72	0	16
(4) All other	91	92	93	100	95
Total	384	380	399	349	376

Addendum:

Average daily holdings of U.S. Securities for March in System Account *excluding* March 16-22*:

$$\frac{272 + 245}{23} = 262$$

(From row (1), columns (b) and (d))

TABLE A.II *(Continued)*

GS' for February = 291 + 91 = 382

(From rows (1) and (4), column (a))

GS' for March = 262 + 95 = 357

(From calculation above and row (4), column (e))

ΔGS' for March = 357 - 382 = -25

* Period of Treasury financing

Sources: Basic data for December, 1923 through December, 1930 from U.S. Federal Reserve Board, *Seventeenth Annual Report*, pp. 52-53; for 1931 from *Eighteenth Annual Report*, p. 52.

TABLE A. III
MEMBER BANK RESERVE AND DEPOSIT DATA FOR CALL DATES, 1923-1928

Year	Call Date	Required Reserves (RR)*	Time Deposits (TD)*	Net Demand Deposits (NDD)*	Total Deposits (D)*	Effective Reserve Ratio (ERR)	Ratio of Net Demand Deposits to Time Deposits (NDD/TD)
1923	Apr. 3	1842	8,085	16,086	24,171	.0762	1.9896
	June 30	1850	8,317	16,065	24,382	.0759	1.9315
	Sept. 14	1830	8,404	15,919	24,323	.0752	1.8942
	Dec. 31	1884	8,586	16,377	24,963	.0755	1.9074
1924	Mar. 31	1873	8,814	16,112	24,926	.0751	1.8280
	June 30	1974	9,110	16,828	25,948	.0761	1.8482
	Oct. 10	2089	9,498	17,804	27,302	.0765	1.8744
	Dec. 31	2161	9,707	18,468	28,175	.0767	1.9025
1925	Apr. 6	2078	10,028	17,708	27,736	.0749	1.7658
	June 30	2151	10,286	18,277	28,563	.0753	1.7768
	Sept. 28	2141	10,372	18,258	28,630	.0748	1.7603
	Dec. 31	2256	10,557	19,260	29,817	.0757	1.8243
1926	Apr. 12	2168	10,855	18,392	29,247	.0741	1.6943
	June 30	2226	11,077	18,805	29,882	.0745	1.6976
	—	—	—	—	—	—	—
	Dec. 31	2250	11,340	18,922	30,262	.0744	1.6686

TABLE A. III
(Continued)

Year	Call Date	Required Reserves (RR)*	Time Deposits (TD)*	Net Demand Deposits (NDD)*	Total Deposits (D)*	Effective Reserve Ratio (ERR)	Ratio of Net Demand Deposits to Time Deposits (NDD/TD)
1927	Mar. 23	2220	11,711	18,542	30,253	.0734	1.5832
	June 30	2313	12,103	19,250	31,353	.0738	1.5905
	Oct. 10	2301	12,348	19,170	31,518	.0730	1.5524
	Dec. 31	2424	12,658	20,104	32,762	.0740	1.5882
1928	Feb. 28	2332	12,813	19,236	32,049	.0728	1.5012
	June 30	2345	13,331	19,191	32,422	.0723	1.4395
	Oct. 3	2312	13,159	18,995	32,154	.0719	1.4434
	Dec. 31	2430	13,212	19,944	33,156	.0733	1.5095

* Data in millions of dollars. — Data for call date unavailable.

Description and sources of data:

Required reserves (RR) — Derived from data on total member bank reserves and excess reserves by subtracting excess from total reserves. *Banking and Monetary Statistics*, p. 395.

Time deposits (TD) - Ibid., pp. 73, 75.

Net demand deposits (NDD) - Ibid.

Total deposits (D) - Sum of TD and NDD.

Effective reserve ratio (ERR) - Equals RR/D.

Ratio of net demand deposits to time deposits (NDD/TD) - Self explanatory.

TABLE A. IV

DERIVATION OF THE EFFECTIVE RESERVE RATIO ON DEMAND DEPOSITS FOR CALL DATES

Year	Call Date	(1) TD/D	(2) .03 x (1)	(3) ERR - minus (2)	(4) NDD/D	ERR_{DD} equals (3)/(4)
1923	Apr. 3	.3344	.0100	.0662	.6656	.0994
	June 30	.3411	.0102	.0657	.6589	.0997
	Sept. 14	.3455	.0104	.0648	.6545	.0990
	Dec. 31	.3439	.0103	.0652	.6561	.0993
1924	Mar. 31	.3536	.0106	.0645	.6464	.0997
	June 30	.3510	.0105	.0656	.6490	.1010
	Oct. 10	.3478	.0104	.0661	.6522	.1013
	Dec. 31	.3445	.0103	.0664	.6555	.1012
1925	Apr. 6	.3615	.0108	.0641	.6385	.1003
	June 30	.3601	.0108	.0645	.6399	.1007
	Sept. 28	.3622	.0109	.0639	.6378	.1001
	Dec. 31	.3540	.0106	.0651	.6460	.1007
1926	Apr. 12	.3711	.0111	.0630	.6289	.1001
	June 30	.3706	.0111	.0634	.6294	.1007
	—	—	—	—	—	—
	Dec. 31	.3747	.0112	.0632	.6253	.1010
1927	Mar. 23	.3871	.0116	.0618	.6129	.1008
	June 30	.3860	.0116	.0622	.6140	.1013
	Oct. 10	.3917	.0118	.0612	.6083	.1006
	Dec. 31	.3863	.0116	.0624	.6137	.1016

TABLE A. IV *(Continued)*

Year	Call Date	(1) TD/D	(2) .03 x (1)	(3) ERR - minus (2)	(4) NDD / D	ERR_{DD} equals (3)/(4)
1928	Feb. 28	.3997	.0120	.0608	.6003	.1012
	June 30	.4111	.0123	.0600	.5889	.1018
	Oct. 3	.4092	.0123	.0596	.5908	.1008
	Dec. 31	.3984	.0120	.0613	.6016	.1018

— Data for call date unavailable. Sources: See Table A. III for sources of basic data.

Description of data:

TD/D Ratio of time deposits (TD) to total deposits (D).

ERR Effective reserve ratio on total deposits.

NDD/D Ratio of net demand deposits (NDD) to total deposits (D).

ERR_{DD} Column (3) / column (4). That this is true may be seen by considering the composition of the effective reserve ratio on total deposits:

$$ERR = \frac{(ERR_{TD} \times TD) + (ERR_{DD} \times NDD)}{D}$$

where ERR_{TD} is the effective reserve ratio on time deposits and the other variables are as previously defined. Substituting the known values of ERR, ERR_{TD} (=.03), TD, NDD, and D allows solution of this equation for ERR_{DD} as above. It might be noted that ERR_{DD} is a weighted average of the reserve ratios required for different classes of banks; the weights being the proportion of Net Demand Deposits held in each class of bank.

TABLE A. V

DERIVATION OF ESTIMATES OF REQUIRED AND EXCESS RESERVES
(April, 1923 - December, 1928)

Year	Month	NDD	TD	D	$\widehat{ERR}$	$\widehat{RR}$	R	$\widehat{ER}$
1923	April	15,800	8,251	24,051	0.0752	1,810	1,854	43
	May	15,893	8,291	24,184	0.0754	1,824	1,931	106
	June	15,756	8,388	24,144	0.0752	1,815	1,868	52
	July	15,708	8,343	24,051	0.0753	1,812	1,839	26
	Aug	15,529	8,436	23,965	0.0750	1,797	1,849	51
	Sept.	15,627	8,473	24,100	0.0751	1,810	1,852	41
	Oct.	15,906	8,526	24,432	0.0754	1,842	1,872	29
	Nov.	15,897	8,568	24,465	0.0753	1,843	1,881	37
	Dec.	15,830	8,576	24,406	0.0753	1,838	1,874	35
1924	Jan.	15,943	8,694	24,637	0.0752	1,854	1,935	80
	Feb.	15,846	8,805	24,651	0.0749	1,848	1,927	78
	March	15,815	8,896	24,711	0.0748	1,848	1,912	63
	April	15,944	8,975	24,919	0.0748	1,864	1,935	70
	May	15,987	9,041	25,028	0.0747	1,871	1,936	64
	June	16,397	9,148	25,545	0.0750	1,917	2,035	117
	July	16,710	9,269	25,979	0.0752	1,953	2,075	121
	Aug.	17,040	9,368	26,408	0.0754	1,991	2,082	90
	Sept.	17,360	9,517	26,877	0.0754	2,028	2,120	91
	Oct.	17,765	9,675	27,440	0.0756	2,075	2,162	86
	Nov.	17,947	9,796	27,743	0.0756	2,097	2,148	50
	Dec.	17,957	9,727	27,684	0.0757	2,098	2,223	124

TABLE A. V *(Continued)*

Year	Month	NDD	TD	D	$\widehat{ERR}$	$\widehat{RR}$	R	$\widehat{ER}$
1925	Jan.	17,927	9,886	27,813	0.0754	2,099	2,141	41
	Feb.	17,888	10,006	27,894	0.0752	2,099	2,208	108
	Mar.	17,503	10,094	27,597	0.0747	2,062	2,119	56
	Apr.	17,715	10,187	27,902	0.0748	2,087	2,163	75
	May	17,552	10,325	27,877	0.0744	2,074	2,138	63
	June	17,671	10,407	28,078	0.0744	2,089	2,140	50
	July	17,817	10,406	28,223	0.0746	2,105	2,161	55
	Aug.	17,840	10,475	28,315	0.0745	2,110	2,183	72
	Sept.	18,005	10,503	28,508	0.0746	2,128	2,207	78
	Oct.	18,432	10,629	29,061	0.0748	2,176	2,227	50
	Nov.	18,371	10,692	29,063	0.0747	2,172	2,220	47
	Dec.	18,443	10,627	29,070	0.0749	2,178	2,219	40
1926	Jan.	18,356	10,803	29,159	0.0745	2,174	2,217	42
	Feb.	18,261	10,880	29,141	0.0743	2,167	2,203	35
	Mar.	18,009	10,970	28,979	0.0740	2,144	2,218	73
	Apr.	18,064	11,048	29,112	0.0739	2,152	2,171	18
	May	18,138	11,102	29,240	0.0739	2,162	2,195	32
	June	18,110	11,177	29,287	0.0738	2,161	2,225	63
	July	18,112	11,281	29,393	0.0736	2,165	2,205	39
	Aug.	18,072	11,313	29,385	0.0735	2,162	2,204	41
	Sept.	18,234	11,352	29,586	0.0737	2,180	2,231	50
	Oct.	18,280	11,402	29,682	0.0736	2,187	2,217	29
	Nov.	18,216	11,438	29,654	0.0735	2,182	2,202	19
	Dec.	18,395	11,430	29,825	0.0737	2,200	2,218	17

TABLE A. V *(Continued)*

Year	Month	NDD	TD	D	$\widehat{ERR}$	$\widehat{RR}$	R	$\widehat{ER}$
1927	Jan.	18,121	11,608	29,729	0.0732	2,178	2,192	13
	Feb.	18,105	11,795	29,900	0.0729	2,182	2,166	-16
	Mar.	18,357	11,900	30,257	0.0730	2,211	2,300	88
	Apr.	18,346	12,002	30,348	0.0729	2,213	2,270	56
	May	18,471	12,124	30,595	0.0728	2,230	2,268	37
	June	18,534	12,159	30,693	0.0729	2,237	2,307	69
	July	18,555	12,261	30,816	0.0727	2,243	2,282	38
	Aug.	18,493	12,334	30,827	0.0726	2,239	2,306	66
	Sept.	18,667	12,452	31,119	0.0726	2,260	2,337	76
	Oct.	18,960	12,527	31,487	0.0728	2,293	2,352	58
	Nov.	19,180	12,579	31,759	0.0729	2,317	2,369	51
	Dec.	19,586	12,677	32,263	0.0732	2,361	2,397	35
1928	Jan.	19,719	12,928	32,647	0.0729	2,383	2,473	89
	Feb.	19,162	12,990	32,152	0.0724	2,328	2,395	66
	Mar.	19,107	13,059	32,166	0.0722	2,325	2,361	35
	Apr.	19,391	13,259	32,650	0.0722	2,360	2,432	71
	May	19,315	13,420	32,735	0.0720	2,358	2,426	67
	June	19,170	13,443	32,613	0.0718	2,344	2,392	47
	July	18,789	13,422	32,211	0.0715	2,305	2,365	59
	Aug.	18,273	13,378	31,651	0.0711	2,252	2,266	13
	Sept.	18,691	13,368	32,059	0.0715	2,294	2,349	54
	Oct.	18,779	13,462	32,241	0.0715	2,306	2,313	6
	Nov.	19,005	13,511	32,516	0.0716	2,331	2,330	-1
	Dec.	19,160	13,418	32,578	0.0719	2,344	2,409	64

* Monthly data on member bank deposits are unavailable prior to April, 1923.

TABLE A. V *(Continued)*

** Data on member bank deposits are available only for the fourth or fifth Wednesday of each month for April, 1923 - October, 1926, and for the first or second Wednesday thereafter. Hence, the data on reserves are taken for the same day. As a result, the estimates of required and excess reserves apply for that same day. It is probably not a drastic departure from reality to take the change in the average figures, however. As previously emphasized, alternative regressions were tried using a defensive variable *not* dependent on these estimates of required reserves as a check on the regressions presented in the body of this study.

Description and sources of data:

NDD Net demand deposits of all member banks in millions of dollars. Data for 1923-1927 from U.S. Federal Reserve Board, *Fourteenth Annual Report*, p. 116; data for 1928 from *Fifteenth Annual Report*, p. 108.

TD Time deposits of all member banks in millions of dollars. Ibid.

D Total deposits of all member banks in millions of dollars. D = NDD + TD.

$\widehat{ERR}$ Estimated effective reserve ratio for total deposits. Estimated from the regression obtained using call date data. (See text and Table A.III.) In multiplicative form this regression is

$$\widehat{ERR}_t = .0637\,(NDD/TD)_t^{.2382}\,(t)^{.0085}.$$

$\widehat{RR}$ Estimated required reserves of all member banks in millions of dollars. $\widehat{RR} = \widehat{ERR} \times D$.

TABLE A. V *(Continued)*

R Actual reserves of all member banks in millions of dollars on same day (or preceding day) as NDD and TD reported. *Banking and Monetary Statistics*, pp. 379-383.

$\widehat{ER}$ Estimated excess reserves in millions of dollars. $\widehat{ER} = R - \widehat{RR}$.

NOTES

1. The required reserve ratio for time deposits was three percent at all classes of member banks. The reserve requirements for demand deposits were thirteen percent at Central Reserve City banks, ten percent at Reserve City banks, and seven percent at County banks. These rates were effective from June 21, 1917 through August 14, 1936. *(Banking and Monetary Statistics,* p. 400.)

Friedman and Schwartz discuss the incentive given to member banks to take advantage of lower reserve requirements on time deposits and the methods used by these banks to induce customers to change from demand to time deposits. (See Friedman and Schwartz, *Monetary History,* pp. 276-278; and the references cited therein.)

2. This was the result of a shift of demand deposits from member banks with relatively low reserve requirements to member banks with higher reserve requirements. This could have, in turn, been the result of the failure of more small banks than larger banks and the response of depositors to same. Whatever the reason, the relative distribution of demand deposits shows an increase in the percent of demand deposits of member banks in Central Reserve Cities while the relative share of demand deposits in Country banks declined. The following table illustrates this point.

Percentage of Total Member Bank Demand Deposits Held by Banks Classified as

End of year*	Central Reserve City	Reserve City	Country
1923	30.6	32.7	36.7
1924	33.4	32.6	34.0
1925	32.9	33.0	34.1
1926	33.5	32.7	33.7
1927	33.8	32.7	33.5
1928	35.7	31.9	32.4

*December 31.

Sources: U.S. Federal Reserve Board, *Eleventh Annual Report*, pp. 124-127; *Twelfth Annual Report*, pp. 139-142; *Thirteenth Annual Report*, p. 149; *Fourteenth Annual Report*, p. 185; *Fifteenth Annual Report*, p. 113.

3. The lack of monthly data for the relative distribution of deposits among classes of member banks excludes the possibility of using this information in calculating the effective required reserve ratio on all deposits. The time trend should capture this effect, however.

APPENDIX B

Spectral Analysis of Selected Components of the Reserve Equation

The results of a spectral analysis of the more important components of the reserve equation[1] are reported in this appendix. This analysis is useful because it contributes to an understanding of the various factors influencing these components; but more importantly, it provides a helpful insight into the basic question posed in this thesis.

The spectral analysis was applied to the first differences[2] of member bank reserves (ΔR); the Federal Reserve Banks' holdings of government securities (ΔGS and $\Delta GS'$), acceptances (ΔA), and bills discounted (ΔB); the monetary stock of gold (ΔG); and currency in circulation (ΔM).[3] The power density spectra of these series are presented for two time periods (1923-1931 and 1923-June 1931, both inclusive) in Charts B.I through B.VII (see pages 163-169).[4] In addition, Chart B.III compares the power density spectra of the two different series on open market purchases and sales (ΔGS and $\Delta GS'$) described in Chapter Three.[5]

An examination of the spectra in these charts leads to interesting conclusions about the nature of the fluctuations in each of the series. Before drawing any broad conclusions from the analysis, each of the spectra is considered separately below. Then the conclusions drawn from all of the spectra are reported.

Seasonal and Cyclical Fluctuations in Each of the Components

Chart B.I contains the power density spectrum for changes in member bank reserves. The occurrence of a peak in the spectrum at (or close to) a period of 12, 6, 4, 3, 2.4, or 2 months is an indication of a seasonal pattern in member bank reserves. However, the seasonal peaks are not particularly strong, and it could be argued that the peaks are not statistically significant as measured by the ninety percent confidence interval indicated on the chart (as on all the subsequent charts). However, the most important point is that there is absolutely no indication of a cyclical pattern (which would show up in the spectrum under examination as a peak at the twenty-or-thirty-month period),[6] especially in the spectrum computed through June, 1931, only. The importance of this point is made clear in the conclusions below.

It is evident from Chart B.II. that purchases and sales of government securities *do* exhibit a cyclical fluctuation. The series does not show any signs of a seasonal pattern, but there does appear to be a recurrent fluctuation with a period of around three months. This result is due to two Federal Reserve operations which have opposite effects. These operations are (1) the sale of securities from the System account in the open market around the fifteenth of March, June, September, and December to absorb funds put into the market by Treasury tax operations, and (2) the purchase of one- and/or two-day certificates directly from the Treasury to provide funds for operation while tax collections take place.[7]

Chart B.III compares the power density spectra for ΔGS with its alternative $\Delta GS'$ which was constructed to exclude tax-related operations.[8] It is apparent from a comparison of the two spectra that this construction was successful in that the power density spectrum of $\Delta GS'$ displays much the same cyclical fluctuation as ΔGS, except for the three-month fluctuation involved in the Treasury operations.

It is important to note, in summary, that purchases and sales of government securities exhibit a cyclical pattern and little or no seasonal pattern; and that the power density spectrum for ΔGS is the same regardless of whether the period is ended in June, 1931, or December, 1931. (The two spectra in Chart B.II are indistinguishable.)

The power density spectrum of the Fed's holdings of acceptances (ΔA) is displayed in Chart B.IV. It is apparent that this series displays a strong seasonal pattern while there is no evidence of a cyclical peak. This is true regardless of which period is used, although the seasonal influence is much more marked when the period is ended in June, 1931.

The power density spectrum of changes in bills discounted at the Fed (ΔB, Chart B.V) is more difficult to interpret, but the series appears to exhibit both a seasonal and a cyclical pattern. Because of the relatively short length of the series (108 observations) and the maximum lag used (30 months), these two peaks are close together and tend to blur into one. Hence it is difficult to determine exactly where the peaks occur.

However, the "alias" peaks (at six, four, three, etc., months) tend to support the conclusion of a seasonal pattern. The rise in the spectrum to a peak prior to twelve months (in fact, at twenty-thirty months) can best be explained as due to cyclical forces. Notice that here, too, the spectrum is virtually the same regardless of which period is employed.

The plot of the power density spectrum of changes in the monetary gold stock (ΔG, Chart B.VI) exhibits a property not evident in any of the spectra examined so far. For the period 1923-1931, there appears to be something of a cyclical pattern, although this is far from certain. For the period 1923 - June 1931 only, the maximum power appears to be concentrated at a period even longer than the cyclical period. This may result from a failure to remove completely the trend in the monetary stock of gold by first differencing. The trend would appear, upon casual inspection, to be upward, but at a decreasing rate, prior to mid-1931. In the last months of that year, the United States experienced a large gold outflow in response to Britain's departure from the gold standard. This seems to have "straightened" the trend somewhat so that first differencing may have at least reduced the major effects of that trend.

Finally, Chart B.VII illustrates what can only be described as a classical seasonal pattern, at least when the period is ended in June, 1931. This is, of course, what is to be expected of changes in currency in circulation (ΔM).

This chart also contains an interesting difference between the spectra calculated for the two different periods. As with changes in member bank reserves (ΔR, Chart B.I), when the period is extended to include the last half of 1931, more power seems to be concentrated in the longer (cyclical or trend) periods. However, when the period is ended in June, 1931, there is absolutely no evidence of a cyclical factor at work.

Conclusions

The spectral analysis of the selected components cannot tell us what causes the observed fluctuations or whether two series exhibiting the same patterns are in any way causally related. What is attempted here, however, is to offer a plausible explanation of the observed patterns based on what was learned in the historical summary in Chapter Two.

The fact that both ΔGS and ΔB exhibit cyclical fluctuations is probably explained by the fact that purchases and sales were undertaken expressly for the purpose of affecting member bank borrowings. The cyclical pattern in ΔGS could be the response of the Fed to cyclical patterns in business activity[9] (or vice-versa) with the cyclical pattern of ΔB indicating a response to ΔGS—an increase in borrowings to defend reserves against sales of government securities by the Fed or a decrease in borrowings permitted by the Fed's purchases.[10]

The only other series that could be interpreted as exhibiting a cyclical factor is ΔG. This could be either a response to changing monetary conditions in the United States, or a motivation for purchases and sales, or both. The spectral analysis of ΔG is the least successful, however, in terms of determining with any degree of certainty the nature of the fluctuations involved.

It is significant that ΔR does *not* exhibit a cyclical pattern, at least not when the period is ended in June, 1931. This means that, up until the last half of 1931, member bank reserves were "cushioned" from cyclical changes. This could be due to the response of member bank borrowings to potential cyclical changes and/or to purchases and sales of government securities by the Federal Reserve System in response to cyclical gold flows (i.e., "sterilization" of gold flows by the Fed).

Both ΔB and ΔA exhibit seasonal fluctuations. It is widely accepted that member banks borrowed to meet seasonal demands for currency (ΔM). It is also known that sales of acceptances by member banks to the Federal Reserve Banks exhibited well-marked seasonal fluctuations in response to the seasonal movements in trade.[11] It seems fair to conclude that member banks used both sales of acceptances and borrowing to provide for seasonal needs arising from changes in other components in the reserve equation (i.e., in "defense" of their reserve position in response to such changes as, for example, ΔM).[12] How much of these operations was "dynamic" rather than "defensive," or geared to expanding their reserve position instead of simply holding it, is impossible to tell from the present analysis.

The most important conclusions drawn from the analysis, however, rest on the differences, or lack of differences, observed in the power density spectra calculated for the two different periods—one ending in June, 1931, the other in December, 1931. As was previously noted, the spectra for ΔR and ΔM appear to exhibit different patterns in the longer periods (the cyclical or trend periods) when the time period is extended to the end of 1931 than when the time period is ended in June of that year. The same is true for ΔG, except that the power in the longer periods is increased by the shortening of the time period. The differences appearing in these spectra are reflections of the large outflow of gold in response to Britain's departure from the gold standard, the increase in currency in circulation because of the banking panic (made worse by Britain's departure from gold), and the decline in member bank reserves which resulted from these changes and the failure of Federal Reserve credit to offset them.[13] The failure of Federal Reserve credit to offset these changes is reflected in the absence of any difference among the spectra for ΔGS, ΔA, and ΔB in the two time periods.

The two earlier recessions in the 1920's were not accompanied by banking panics. The power spectrum for ΔM, even in the period up to the summer of 1931, shows no cyclical fluctuations. But after the summer of 1931, currency in circulation rose rapidly.

The present analysis can be interpreted as supporting Friedman and Schwartz's conclusion that the Fed's biggest failure was to recognize the liquidity crisis for what it was and to respond with large purchases of government securities. There was no provision of credit to member banks of the magnitude required to offset the outflow of gold and the increase in currency in circulation. Borrowings rose in spite of higher discount rates; but, as Friedman and Schwartz have stated:

> [t]he aversion to borrowing by banks which the Reserve System had tried to strengthen during the twenties, was still greater at a time when depositors were fearful for the safety of every bank and were scrutinizing balance sheets with great care to see which banks were likely to be the next to go.[14]

As a result, member bank reserves fell at a time when a restoration of confidence might have been made possible by increasing these reserves.

Summary

The spectral analysis reported in this appendix indicates a cyclical factor in both ΔGS and ΔB throughout the entire period 1923-1931. The spectral analysis of member bank reserves indicates that reserves did *not* exhibit a cyclical behavior prior to the summer of 1931. Their decline after that time is attributable to the loss of gold and the increase in currency in circulation which were not offset by increases in Federal Reserve Bank credit.

It was the failure of the Federal Reserve System to respond to the developments in the last half of 1931 that represents the most "inconsistent" behavior, based on the spectral analysis. But this "inconsistency" is probably the result of a lack of experience with any situation even remotely similar. Hence the label "inconsistent" is questionable at best.

Finally, the similarity of the spectra for ΔGS in 1923-1931 and 1923 - June, 1931, and the similarity of the spectra for ΔB in the same two periods, are indications that Federal Reserve policy did not respond to the needs of the last half of 1931. Member bank borrowing rose "on schedule" in spite of a continuing recession. Purchases of government securities, too, were "on schedule" with recovery, only there was no recovery.

Chart B.I

Power Density Spectrum of ΔR

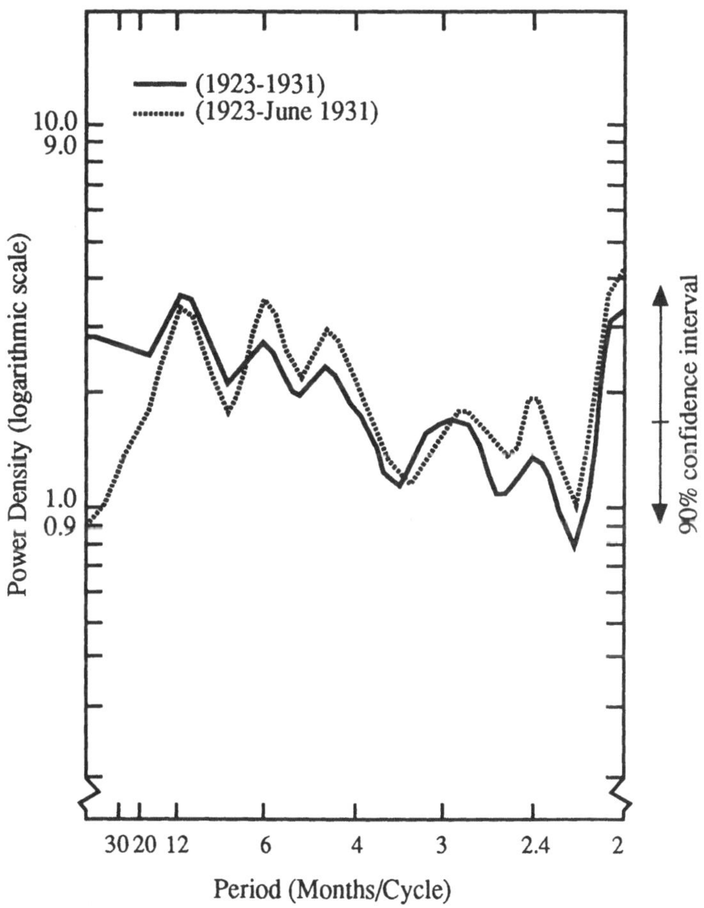

Chart B.II

Power Density Spectrum of ΔGS

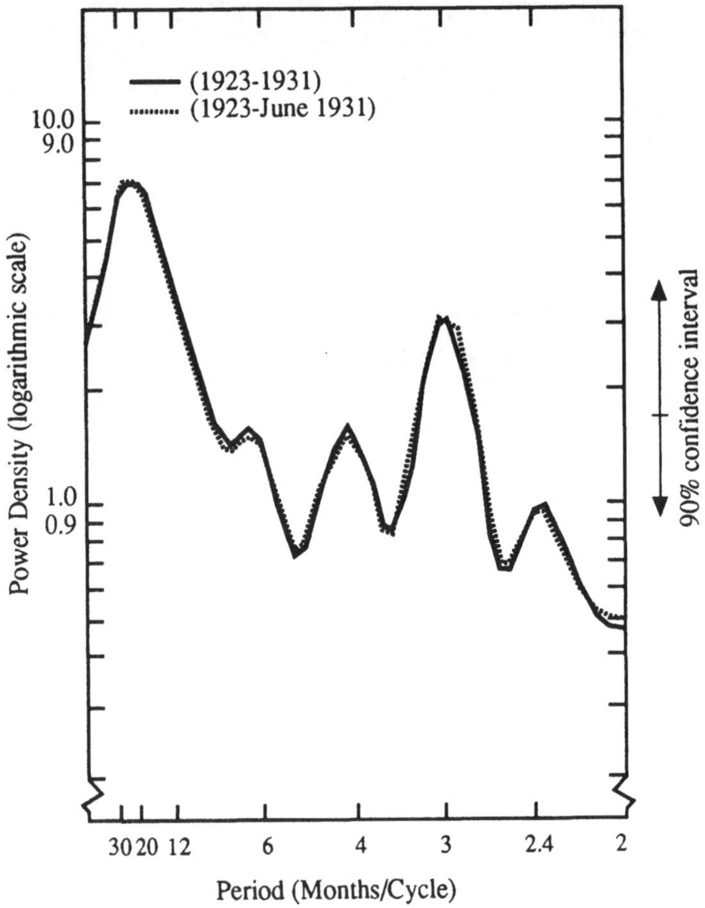

Chart B.III

Power Density Spectra of
ΔGS
ΔGS'
(1924-1931)

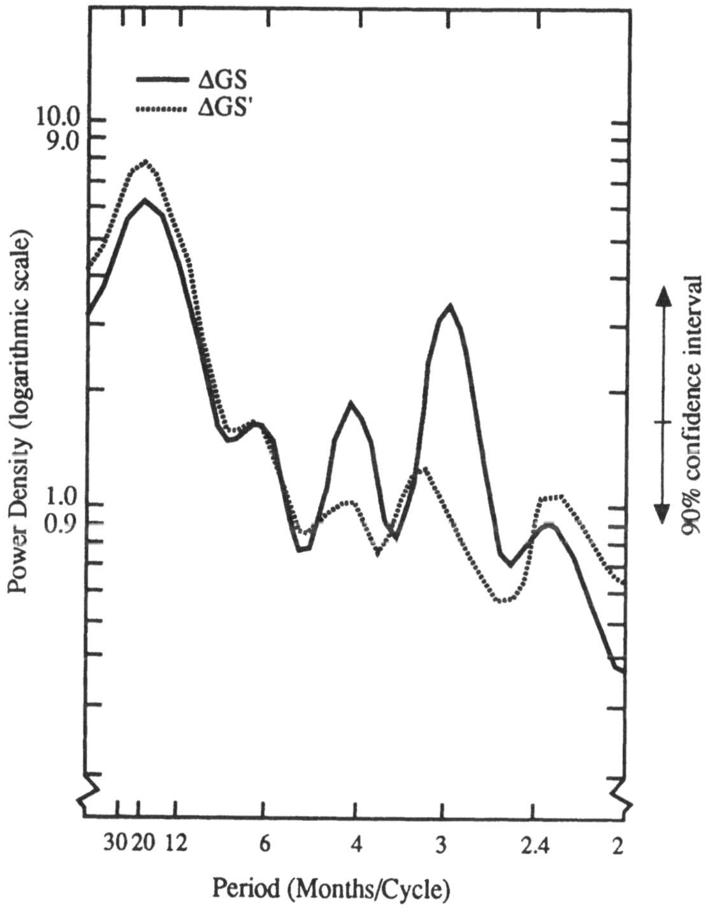

Chart B.IV

Power Density Spectrum of ΔA

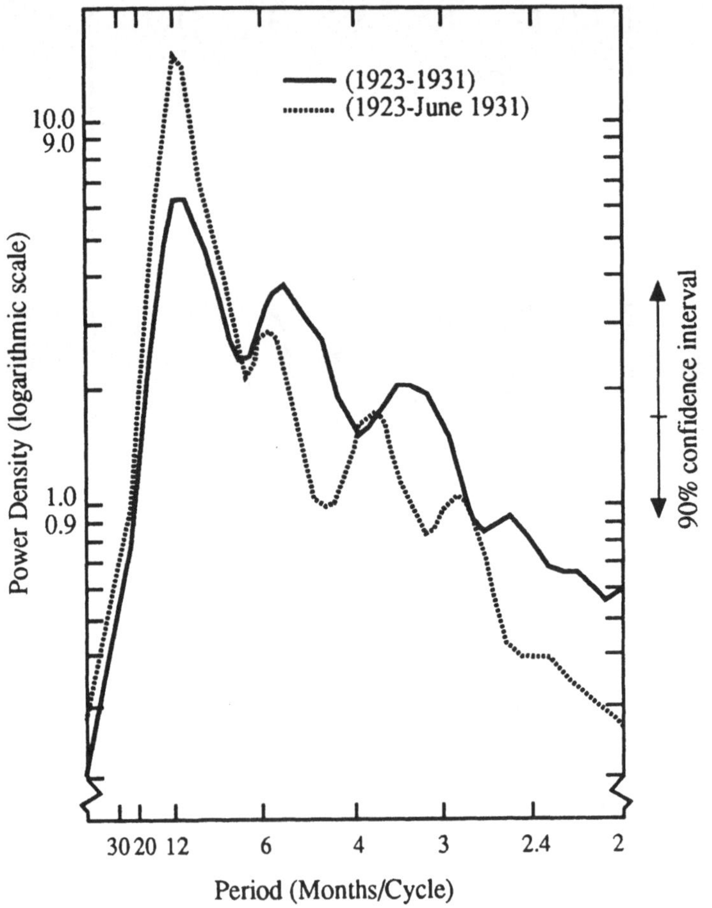

Chart B.V

Power Density Spectrum of ΔB

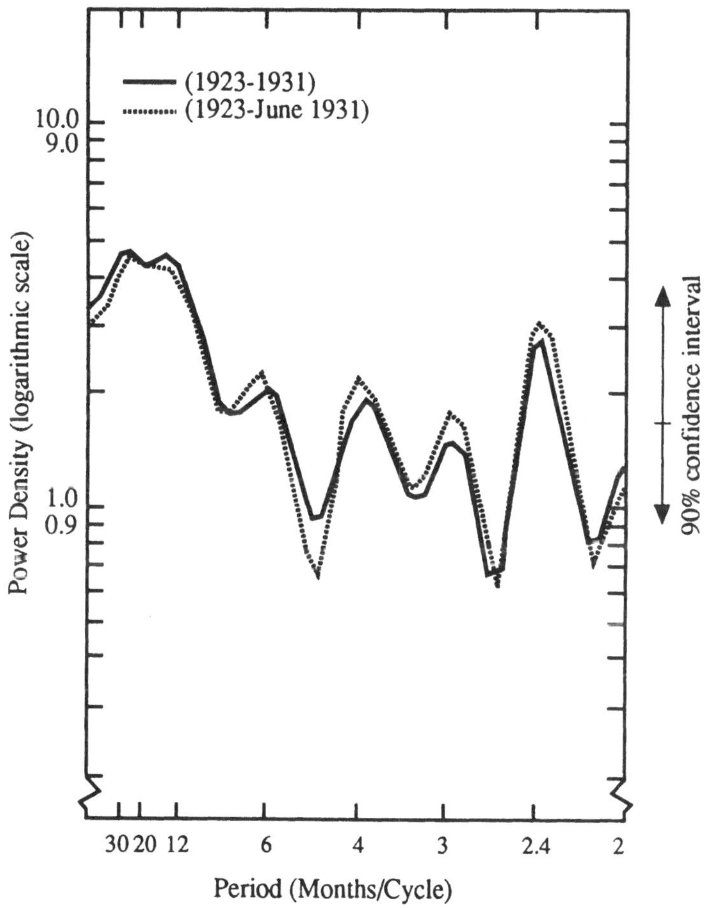

Chart B.VI

Power Density Spectrum of ΔG

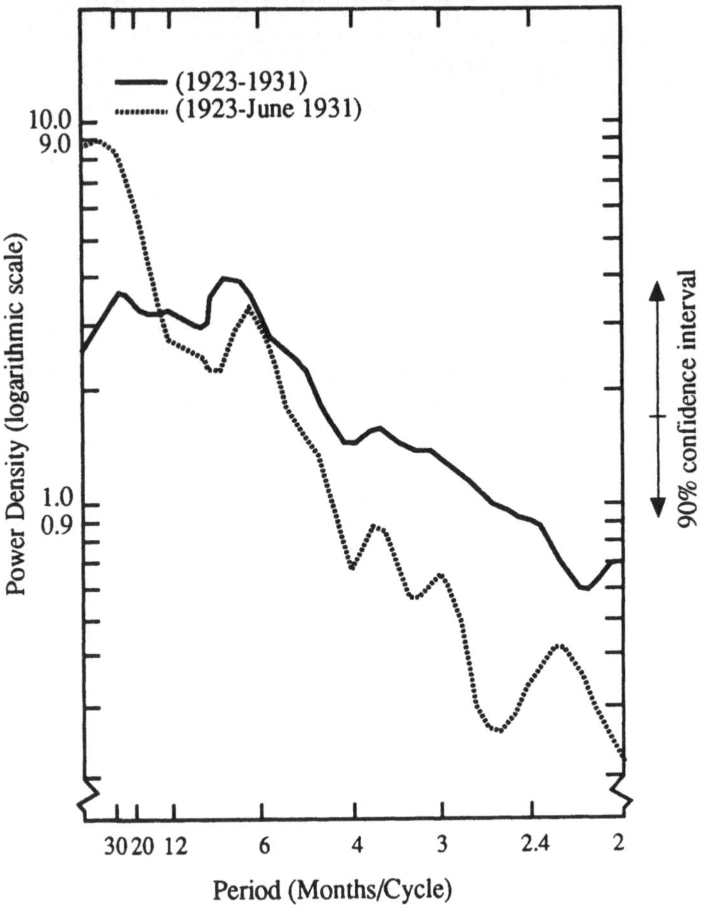

Chart B.VII

Power Density Spectrum of ΔM

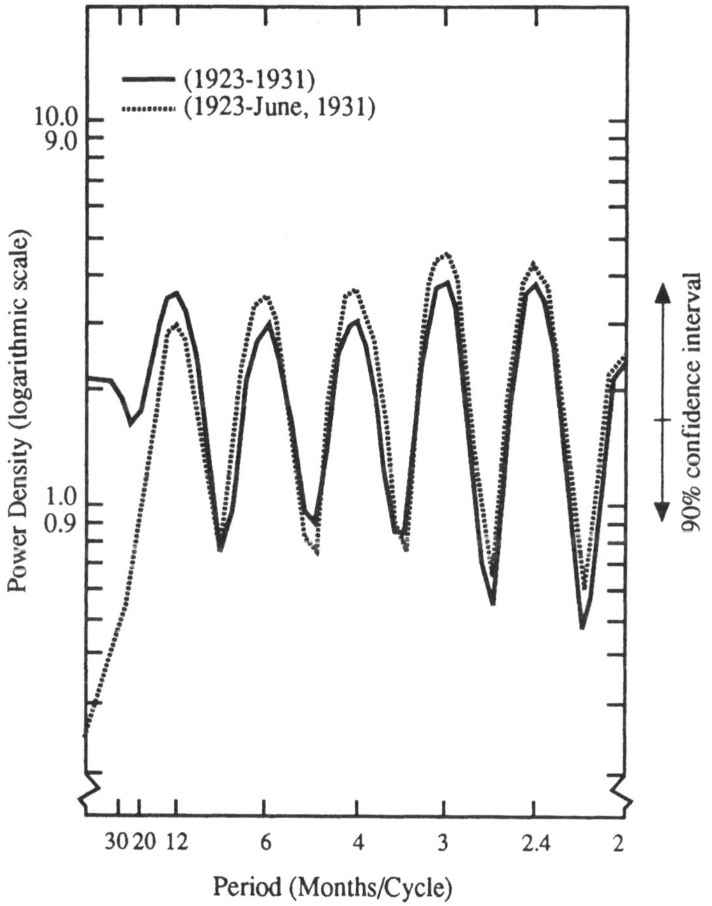

NOTES

1. The reserve equation is the algebraic statement that the factors supplying reserve funds (sources) are equal to the factors absorbing these funds (uses). Alternatively, the equation may be thought of as defining the reserve position of member banks. The reserve equation is important precisely because it shows how the volume of member bank reserves is determined. These reserves are, of course, the basis for the extension of member bank credit.

For a complete discussion of the reserve equation, see U.S. Board of Governors of the Federal Reserve System, *The Federal Reserve System: Purposes and Functions* (Washington, D.C.: U.S. Board of Governors, 1963), pp. 199-224; or, *Banking and Monetary Statistics*, pp. 360-366.

2. First differences were used for two reasons: (1) we are primarily interested in the changes in each of these components, and (2) first-differencing removes a linear trend. The removal of the trend factor is desirable for technical reasons. The interested reader is referred to Gwilym M. Jenkins and Donald G. Watts, *Spectral Analysis and Its Applications* (San Francisco: Holden-Day, 1968), pp. 147-152.

3. These are the most important components of the reserve equation from our point of view. The factors other than reserves happen also to be the most important sources of fluctuations in reserves and are therefore the most important in that sense. A spectral analysis of the sum of all other components (except "other" Federal Reserve credit, mainly float), indicates little, if any, regular fluctuation in this sum. It appears to contain mainly random fluctuations.

"Other" Federal Reserve credit exhibits a three-month cycle. This is probably due to the increase in float in months in which treasury operations related to taxes and refunding occur. More is said about these operations later.

4. In the calculations of the spectra, a maximum lag of thirty months was used. This length was chosen to be as long as the total length of the series would allow to insure greater detail in the spectra. A

problem still arises, as is evident from the subsequent discussion in the text of this appendix, where a series contains both seasonal and cyclical elements.

5. As a reminder, ΔGS is the first difference in the average daily holdings of government securities by the System as a whole. This, therefore, includes one-day treasury certificates and purchases made under resale agreement. ΔGS' excludes the latter two elements and was obtained in such a way that it does not include operations designed to offset the Treasury operations, previously mentioned, that usually occurred around the middle of March, June, September, and December.

6. The usual length of the business cycle is considered to be three or three and one-half years (or, thirty-six to forty-two months). This is certainly true in the period under examination. However, the use of maximum lag of thirty months (desirable for the greater detail it permits, but limited by the length of the series) excludes the possibility of obtaining a peak at thirty-six - forty-two months. This does not, however, mean that a cyclical fluctuation cannot be detected.

Power density spectra typically exhibit what is known as "aliasing." This means that the power density spectrum of a series that exhibits, say, a seasonal fluctuation will contain peaks not only at twelve months, but possibly also at six months, four months, and so on. The latter peaks are "aliases" of the true peak. Chart B.VII, showing the power density spectrum of ΔM, illustrates this point beautifully.

Hence, a cyclical fluctuation of, say, forty months, would probably show up also at twenty months in the power spectrum. This is what happens in the series under examination.

7. See Chapter Three. The references cited there are Burgess, *Federal Reserve Policy and Benjamin Strong*, pp. 99-103; Hardy, *Credit Policies*, pp. 68-69; and *Excerpts*, pp. 13, 17, 47.

8. The spectra are calculated for both ΔGS and ΔGS' over the period 1924-1931 because the latter series is not available before 1924. See Chapter Three and Appendix A.

9. The coincidence of the international and domestic goals during the recessions of 1923-1924 and 1926-1927 means that a cyclical pattern in purchases and sales could have been the result of the pursuit of international as well as (or instead of) domestic goals. The decision between the two is made in Chapter Three.

10. This interpretation is supported by an observed negative simple correlation between ΔB and ΔGS of -.24. In addition, the coherence between the two series is approximately .59 at the cyclical period. (Coherence may be roughly thought of as similar to the coefficient of determination between two variables, but restricted to one frequency or period.)

11. See, for example, Burgess, *Federal Reserve Policy and Benjamin Strong*, pp. 48-53, 131-136.

12. The simple correlation coefficient between ΔA and the sum of all other changes in sources less uses other than reserves is -.88. The corresponding correlation coefficient for ΔB is -.93. This tends to support the belief that changes in acceptances sold and bills discounted were largely "defensive" operations.

13. See Table A.I., Appendix A for the relevant data.

14. Friedman and Schwartz, *Monetary History*, pp. 318-319.

APPENDIX C

Minimization of the Disutility Function

This appendix contains the mathematical procedures in minimizing the disutility functions of Chapter Three. The general procedure is described in that chapter.

Model I

$$d_t = w_1 (r_t - r_t^*)^2 + w_2 (\Delta GS_t)^2 + w_3 (\Delta dr_t)^2 + w_4 (\Delta ar_t)^2 \qquad \text{(I.1.a)}$$

$$r_t = l_0 + l_1 O_t + l_2 SS_t + l_3 \Delta B_t + l_4 B_{t-1} + l_5 \Delta dr_t$$

$$+ l_6 dr_{t-1} + l_7 \Delta ar_t + l_8 ar_{t-1} \qquad \text{(I.2.b)}$$

$$\Delta B_t = c_0 + c_1 \Delta N_t - c_2 \Delta dr_{t-1} + c_3 \Delta ar_{t-1} \qquad \text{(I.3)}$$

$$\Delta N_t \equiv \Delta RR'_t - \Delta GS_t \qquad \text{(I.4.a)}$$

$$r_t^* = d_0 + d_1 O_t + d_2 SC_t + d_3 SS_t + d_4 r_{L_t} \qquad \text{(I.5)}$$

Substituting (I.4.a) into (I.3) yields

$$\Delta B_t = c_0 + c_1 \Delta RR'_t - c_1 \Delta GS_t - c_2 \Delta dr_{t-1} + c_3 \Delta ar_{t-1} \qquad \text{(I.3.a)}$$

Substituting this result into (I.2.b) yields

$$r_t = l_0 + l_1O_t + l_2SS_t + l_3c_1\ \Delta RR'_t + l_3C_0$$

$$-l_3c_1\ \Delta GS_t - l_3c_2\ \Delta dr_{t-1} + l_3c_3\ \Delta ar_{t-1}$$

$$+ l_4B_{t-1} + l_5\ \Delta dr_t + l_6\ dr_{t-1} + l_7\ \Delta ar_t + l_8\ ar_{t-1} \qquad \text{(I.2.c)}$$

By substituting (I.2.c) and (I.5) into (I.1.a), taking the derivative with respect to each of the policy variables, setting the results equal to zero, and then solving for each of the policy variables, we can find those values of the policy variables that insure the minimum disutility. It is simpler, however, to take the derivatives of the disutility function first and then substitute. This is done below.

Open market operations.

$$\frac{\partial d_t}{\partial \Delta GS_t} = 2w_1r_t\frac{\partial r_t}{\partial \Delta GS_t} - 2w_1r_t{*}\ \frac{\partial r_t}{\partial \Delta GS_t} + 2w_2\ \Delta GS_t$$

Substituting $\dfrac{\partial r_t}{\partial \Delta GS_t} = -\ l_3c_1$ into the above and setting the result equal to zero yields

$$0 = -2w_1l_3c_1r_t + 2w_1l_3c_1r_t{*} + 2w_2\ \Delta GS_t$$

Let $g_1 = l_3c_1$ for simplicity, divide by two, and we have

$$0 = -w_1g_1r_t + w_1g_1r_t{*} + w_3\ \Delta GS_t$$

Substituting (I.2.c) and (I.5) into the above yields

$$0 = -w_1g_1\ (l_0 + l_1O_t + l_2SS_t + l_3c_0$$

$$+ l_3c_1\ \Delta RR'_t - l_3c_1\ \Delta GS_t - l_3c_2\ \Delta dr_{t-1}$$

$$+ l_3 c_3 \Delta ar_{t-1} + l_4 B_{t-1} + l_5 \Delta dr_t$$

$$+ l_6 dr_{t-1} + l_7 \Delta ar_t + l_8 ar_{t-1})$$

$$+ w_1 g_1 (d_0 + d_1 O_t + d_2 SC_t + d_3 SS_t$$

$$+ d_4 r_{Lt}) + w_2 \Delta GS_t$$

$$0 = (-w_1 g_1 l_0 - w_1 g_1 l_3 c_0 + w_1 g_1 d_0)$$

$$- (w_1 g_1 l_1 - w_1 g_1 d_1) O_t$$

$$- (w_1 g_1 l_2 - w_1 g_1 d_3) SS_t$$

$$- w_1 g_1 l_3 c_1 \Delta RR'_t$$

$$+ w_1 g_1 l_3 c_1 \Delta GS_t$$

$$+ w_1 g_1 l_3 c_3 \Delta dr_{t-1}$$

$$- w_1 g_1 l_3 c_3 \Delta ar_{t-1}$$

$$- w_1 g_1 l_4 B_{t-1} - w_1 g_1 l_5 \Delta dr_t$$

$$- w_1 g_1 l_6 dr_{t-1} - w_1 g_1 l_7 \Delta ar_t$$

$$- w_1 g_1 l_8 ar_{t-1}$$

$$+ w_1 g_1 d_2 SC_t + w_1 g_1 d_4 r_{Lt} + w_2 \Delta GS_t$$

Solving for ΔGS_t yields

$$- (w_1 g_1 l_3 c_1 + w2) \Delta GS_t = \ldots$$

Letting $D_1 = -(w_1g_1l_3c_1 + w_2)$ and dividing by D_1 yields the results, in simplified form,

$$\Delta GS_t = \pm A_0 - A_1O_t - A_2SS_t + A_3\,\Delta RR'_t$$

$$- A_4SC_t - A_5r_{L_t} - A_6\,\Delta dr_{t-1}$$

$$+ A_7\,\Delta ar_{t-1} + A_8\,\Delta dr_t + A_9\,\Delta ar_t$$

$$+ A_{10}B_{t-1} + A_{11}dr_{t-1} + A_{12}ar_{t-1} \qquad \text{(I.6)}$$

The signs of the coefficients of O_t and SS_t have been treated as negative in this result. Actually, the signs are indeterminate from the derivation of (I.6). This is because r_t varies directly with O_t and SS_t, so that an increase in either of the latter would automatically bring about an increase in r_t, which would in turn stimulate purchases (ceteris paribus).

However, at the same time that the increase in O_t and SS_t brought about a higher r_t, if we assume a countercyclical policy (as we have) and a policy designed to offset stock market speculation, then Federal Reserve officials would desire a *further* increase in r_t to counteract the exogenous increases in O_t and SS_t.

The signs of A_1 and A_2 depend on which of the above effects is greater. The negative signs of A_1 and A_2 in (I.6) indicate the belief that the latter effects (due to the countercyclical and antispeculative goals) dominate.

Changes in the discount rate. The procedure here is the same as before except that this time the derivative is taken with respect to Δdr_t.

$$\frac{\partial d_t}{\partial \Delta dr_t} = 2w_1r_t\,\frac{\partial r_t}{\partial \Delta dr_t} - 2w_1r_1 * \frac{\partial r_t}{\partial \Delta dr_t} + 2w_3\Delta dr_t$$

Since $\frac{\partial r_t}{\partial \Delta dr_t} = l_5$, we have

$$0 = 2w_1l_5r_t - 2w_1l_5r_t^* + 2w_3\,\Delta dr_t$$

$$= w_1l_5\,(l_0 + l_1O_t + l_2SS_t + l_3c_0$$

$$+ l_3c_1\,\Delta N_t - l_3c_2\,\Delta dr_{t-1} + l_3c_3\,\Delta ar_{t-1}$$

$$+ l_4B_{t-1} + l_5\,\Delta dr_t + l_6dr_{t-1} + l_7\,\Delta ar_t$$

$$+ l_8ar_{t-1}) - w_1l_5\,(d_0 + d_1O_t + d_2\,SC_t$$

$$+ d_3SS_t + d_4r_{L_t}) + w_3\,\Delta dr_t$$

$$= (w_1l_5l_0 + w_1l_5l_3c_0 - w_1l_5d_0)$$

$$+ (w_1l_5l_1 - w_1l_5d_1)\,O_t + (w_1l_5l_2 - w_1l_5d_3)\,SS_t$$

$$+ (w_1l_5l_3c_1)\,\Delta N_t - (w_1l_5l_3c_2)\,\Delta dr_{t-1}$$

$$+ (w_1l_5l_3c_3)\,\Delta ar_{t-1} + (w_1l_5l_4)\,B_{t-1} + (w_1l_5l_5)\Delta drt$$

$$+ (w_1l_5l_6)\,dr_{t-1} + (w_1l_5l_7)\,\Delta ar_t + (w_1l_5l_8)\,ar_{t-1}$$

$$- (w_1l_5d_2)\,SC_t - (w_1l_5d_4)\,r_{L_t} + w_3\,\Delta dr_t$$

Solving for Δdrt yields

$$- (w_1l_5^2 + w_3)\,\Delta dr_t = \ldots$$

Letting $D2 = -(w_1l_5^2 + w_3)$ and dividing through D_2 yields

$$\Delta dr_t = \pm\,B_0 + B_1O_t + B_2SS_t - B_3\,\Delta N_t$$

$$+ B_4SC_t + B_5r_{Lt} + B_6\,\Delta dr_{t-1}$$

$$- B_7\,\Delta ar_{t-1} - B_8\,\Delta ar_t$$

$$- B_9B_{t-1} - B_{10}dr_{t-1} - B_{11}ar_{t-1} \qquad (I.7)$$

Again, as with the solution for open market operations, the signs of the coefficients O_t and SS_t are actually indeterminate, and for the same reason. It is again assumed that the countercyclical and antispeculative goals outweigh the impact of O_t and SS_t on the rate of interest.

Changes in the acceptance rate. The derivative of (I.1.a) is now taken with respect to Δar_t.

$$\frac{\partial d_t}{\partial \Delta ar_t} = 2w_1r_t\frac{\partial r_t}{\partial \Delta ar_t} - 2w_1r_1 * \frac{\partial r_t}{\partial \Delta ar_t} + 2w_4\Delta ar_t$$

Where $\dfrac{\partial r_t}{\partial \Delta ar_t} = 17$

Since the procedure is once again the same, only the results are presented.

$$\Delta ar_t = \pm\, C_0 + C_1O_t + C_2SS_t - C_3\,\Delta N_t$$

$$+ C_4SC_t + C_5r_{L_t} + C_6\,\Delta dr_{t-1}$$

$$- C_7\,\Delta ar_{t-1} - C_8\,\Delta dr_t$$

$$- C_9B_{t-1} - C_{10}\,dr_{t-1} - C_{11}\,ar_{t-1} \qquad (I.8)$$

The reasoning for the signs of C_1 and C_2 is as before.

Model II

The disutility function and the model with which it is assumed the Fed was working (described in Chapter Three) are repeated below.

$$d_t = w_1 (SS_t)^2 + w_2 (SC_t)^2 + w_3 (\Delta G_t - \Delta G_t^*)^2$$

$$-w_4 (O_{t+K})^2 + w_5 (\Delta GS_t)^2 + w_6 (\Delta dr_t)^2 + w_7 (\Delta ar_t)^2 \qquad (II.1)$$

$$r_t = l_0 + l_1 O_1 + l_2 SS_{t-1} + l_3 S\dot{P}_t + l_4 \Delta B_t + l_5 B_{t-1}$$

$$+ l_6 \Delta dr_t + l_7 dr_{t-1} + l_8 \Delta ar_t + l_9 ar_{t-1} \qquad (II.2)$$

$$\Delta B_t = c_0 + c_1 \Delta N_t - c_2 \Delta dr_{t-1} + c_3 \Delta ar_{t-1} \qquad (II.3)$$

$$\Delta N_t \equiv \Delta RR_t - \Delta S_t^B + \Delta U_t^R \qquad (II.4)$$

$$\Delta N_t \equiv \Delta RR_t' - \Delta GS_t \qquad (II.4.a)$$

$$(\Delta RR_t' \equiv \Delta RR_t - \Delta S_t^{B.\ GS} + \Delta U_t^R)$$

$$SS_t = b_{10} + b_{11} SS_{t-1} - b_{12} r_t + b_{13} S\dot{P}_t \qquad (II.5)$$

$$SC_t = b_{20} + b_{21} SC_{t-1} - b_{22} r_t + b_{23} \dot{P}_t \qquad (II.6)$$

$$\Delta G_t = b_{30} + b_{31} \Delta G_{t-1} b_{32} (r_t - r_{Lt}) + b_{33} BT_t \qquad (II.7)$$

$$\Delta G_t^* = a_{30} - a_{31} G_{t-1} + a_{32} ERS_t - a_{33} DG_t \qquad (II.8)$$

$$O_{t+k} = b40 + b41 O_t - b42 r_t + b43 \dot{P}_t \qquad (II.9)$$

The minimization procedure is the same as before. Substituting (II.4.a) into (II.3) and the result into (II.2) yields

$$r_t = l_0 + l_1O_t + l_2SS_{t-1} + l_3\dot{SP}_t + l_4c_0 + l_4c_1\,\Delta RR_t' - l_4c_1\,\Delta GS_t$$

$$- l_4c_2\,\Delta dr_{t-1} + l_4c_3\,\Delta ar_{t-1} + l_5B_{t-1} + l_6\,\Delta dr_t$$

$$+ l_7dr_{t-1} + l_8\,\Delta ar_t + l_9ar_{t-1} \qquad \text{(II.2.c)}$$

The remainder of the minimization process follows, as before.

Open Market operations:

$$\frac{\partial d_t}{\partial \Delta GS_t} = 2w_1SS_t\frac{\partial SS_t}{\partial \Delta GS_t} + 2w_2SC_t\frac{\partial SC_t}{\partial \Delta GS_t}$$

$$+ 2w_3\,\Delta G_t\frac{\partial \Delta G_t}{\partial \Delta GS_t} - 2w_3\Delta G_t^*\frac{\partial \Delta G_t}{\partial \Delta GS_t}$$

$$- 2w_4O_{t+k}\frac{\partial O_{t+k}}{\partial \Delta GS_t} + 2w_5\Delta GS_t$$

The relevant partial derivatives are

$$\frac{\partial SS_t}{\partial \Delta GS_t} = b12l3c1 \equiv g1 \qquad \frac{\partial SC_t}{\partial \Delta GS_t} = b22l3c1 \equiv g2$$

$$\frac{\partial \Delta G_t}{\partial \Delta GS_t} = -b32l3c1 \equiv -g3 \qquad \frac{\partial O_{t+k}}{\partial \Delta GS_t} = b42l3c1 \equiv g4$$

Substituting the partials into the derivative equation, setting it equal to zero, and dividing by two yields

$$0 = w_1g_1SS_t + w_2g_2SC_t - w_3g_3\,\Delta G_t + w_3g_3\,\Delta G_t^*$$

$$-w_4g_4O_{t+k} + w_5\,\Delta GS_t$$

Substituting for the actual and desired target variables and using equation (II.2) for r_t yields

$$0 = w_1 g_1 (b_{10} + b_{11} SS_{t-1} - b_{12} l_0 - b_{12} l_1 O_t$$

$$- b_{12} l_2 SS_{t-1} - b_{12} l_3 \dot{S}P_t - b_{12} l_4 c_0 - b_{12} l_4 c_1 \Delta RR_t'$$

$$+ b_{12} l_4 c_1 \Delta GS_t + b_{12} l_4 c_2 \Delta dr_{t-1} - b_{12} l_4 c_3 \Delta ar_{t-1}$$

$$- b_{12} l_5 B_{t-1} - b_{12} l_6 \Delta dr_t - b_{12} l_7 dr_{t-1} - b_{12} l_8 \Delta ar_t$$

$$- b_{12} l_9 ar_{t-1} + b_{13} \dot{S}P_t)$$

$$+ w_2 g_2 (b_{20} + b_{21} SC_{t-1} - b_{22} l_0 - b_{22} l_1 O_t$$

$$- b_{22} l_2 SS_{t-1} - b_{22} l_3 \dot{S}P_t - b_{22} l_4 c_0 - b_{22} l_4 c_1 \Delta RR_t'$$

$$+ b_{22} l_4 c_1 \Delta GS_t + b_{22} l_4 c_2 \Delta dr_{t-1} - b_{22} l_4 c_3 \Delta ar_{t-1}$$

$$- b_{22} l_5 B_{t-1} - b_{22} l_6 \Delta dr_t - b_{22} l_7 dr_{t-1} - b_{22} l_8 \Delta ar_t$$

$$- b_{22} l_9 ar_{t-1} + b_{23} \dot{P}_t)$$

$$- w_3 g_3 (b_{30} + b_{31} \Delta G_{t-1} + b_{32} l_0 + b_{32} l_1 O_t$$

$$+ b_{32} l_2 SS_{t-1} + b_{32} l_3 \dot{S}P_t + b_{32} l_4 c_0 + b_{32} l_4 c_1 \Delta RR_t'$$

$$- b_{32} l_4 c_1 \Delta GS_t - b_{32} l_4 c_2 \Delta dr_{t-1} + b_{32} l_4 c_3 \Delta ar_{t-1}$$

$$+ b_{32} l_5 B_{t-1} + b_{32} l_6 \Delta dr_t + b_{32} l_7 dr_{t-1} + b_{32} l_8 \Delta ar_t$$

$$+ b_{32} l_9 ar_{t-1} - b_{32} r_{L_t} + b_{33} BT_t)$$

$$+ w_3 g_3 (a_{30} - a_{31} G_{t-1} + a_{32} ERS_t - a_{33} DG_t)$$

$$- w_4g_4 (b_{40} + b_{41}O_t - b_{42}l_0 - b_{42}\, l_1O_t$$

$$- b_{42}l_2SS_{t-1} - b_{42}l_3\dot{S}P_t - b_{42}l_4c_0 - b_{42}l_4c_1\, \Delta RR_t'$$

$$+ b_{42}l_4c_1\, \Delta GS_t + b_{42}l_4c_2\, \Delta dr_{t-1} - b_{42}l_4c_3\, \Delta ar_{t-1}$$

$$- b_{42}l_5B_{t-1} - b_{42}l_6\, \Delta dr_t - b_{42}l_7dr_{t-1} - b_{42}l_8\, \Delta ar_t$$

$$- b_{42}l_9ar_{t-1} + b_{43}\dot{P}_t)$$

$$+ w_5\, \Delta GS_t$$

Collecting terms and simplifying yields

$$0 = (w_1g_1b_{10} - w_1g_1b_{12}l_0 - w_1g_1b_{12}l_4c_0 + w_2g_2b_{20}$$

$$- w_2g_2b_{22}l_0 - w_2g_2b_{22}l_4c_0 - w_3g_3b_{30}$$

$$- w_3g_3b_{32}l_0 - w_3g_3b_{32}l_4c_0 + w_3g_3a_{30}$$

$$- w_4g_4b_{40} + w_4g_4b_{42}l_0 + w_4g_4b_{42}l_4c_0)$$

$$+ (w_1g_1b_{11} - w_1g_1b_{12}l_2 - w_2g_2b_{22}l_2 - w_3g_3b_{32}l_2$$

$$+ w_4g_4b_{42}l_2)\, SS_{t-1}$$

$$+ (-w_1g_1b_{12}l_1 - w_2g_2b_{22}l_1 - w_3g_3b_{32}l_1 + w_4g_4b_{42}l_1$$

$$+ w_4g_4b_{41})O_t$$

$$+ (-w_1g_1b_{12}l_3 - w_2g_2b_{22}l_3 - w_3g_3b_{32}l_3 + w_4g_4b_{42}l_3$$

$$+ w_1g_1b_{13})\, \dot{S}P_t$$

$$- (w_1 g_1 b_{12} l_4 c_1 + w_2 g_2 b_{22} l_4 c_1 + w_3 g_3 b_{32} l_4 c_1$$

$$-w_4 g_4 b_{42} l_4 c_1)\ \Delta RR_t'$$

$$+ (w_1 g_1 b_{12} l_4 c_1 + w_2 g_2 b_{22} l_4 c_1 + w_3 g_3 b_{32} l_4 c_1$$

$$+ w_5 - w_4 g_4 b_{42} l_4 c_1)\ \Delta GS_t$$

$$+ (w_1 g_1 b_{12} l_4 c_2 + w_2 g_2 b_{22} l_4 c_2 + w_3 g_3 b_{32} l_4 c_2$$

$$- w_4 g_4 b_{42} l_4 c_2)\ \Delta dr_{t-1}$$

$$- (w_1 g_1 b_{12} l_4 c_3 + w_2 g_2 b_{22} l_4 c_3 + w_3 g_3 b_{32} l_4 c_3$$

$$- w_4 g_4 b_{42} l_4 c_3)\ \Delta ar_{t-1}$$

$$- (w_1 g_1 b_{12} l_5 + w_2 g_2 b_{22} l_5 + w_3 g_3 b_{32} l_5$$

$$-w_4 g_4 b_{42} l_5)\ B_{t-1}$$

$$- (w_1 g_1 b_{12} l_6 - w_2 g_2 b_{22} l_6 + w_3 g_3 b_{32} l_6$$

$$- w_4 g_4 b_{42} l_6)\ \Delta dr_t$$

$$- (w_1 g_1 b_{12} l_7 + w_2 g_2 b_{22} l_7 + w_3 g_3 b_{32} l_7$$

$$- w_4 g_4 b_{42} l_7)\ dr_{t-1}$$

$$- (w_1 g_1 b_{12} l_8 + w_2 g_2 b_{22} l_8 + w_3 g_3 b_{32} l_8$$

$$- w_4 g_4 b_{42} l_8)\ \Delta ar_t$$

$$- (w_1 g_1 b_{12} l_9 + w_2 g_2 b_{22} l_9 + w_3 g_3 b_{32} l_9$$

$$- w_4g_4b_{32}l_9)\ ar_{t-1}$$

$$+ (w_2g_2b_{21})\ SC_{t-1} + (w_3g_3b_{32})\ r_{Lt} - (w_3g_3b_{33})\ BT_t$$

$$+ (w_2g_2b_{32} - w_4g_4b_{43})\ \dot{P}_t - (w_3g_3b_{31})\ \Delta G_{t-1}$$

$$- (w_3g_3a_{31})\ G_{t-1} + (w_3g_3a_{32})\ ERS_t - (w_3g_3a_{33})\ DG_t$$

If we subtract the term in ΔGS_t from both sides, we get

$$- (w_1g_1b_{12}l_4c_1 + w_2g_2b_{22}l_4c_1 + w_3g_3b_{32}l_4c_1$$

$$- w_4g_4b_{42}l_4c_1 + w_5)\ \Delta GS_t = \ldots$$

The question of whether the coefficient on ΔGSt is positive or negative depends upon (1) the relative importance of achieving the goals of no speculation in stocks or commodities and the desired gold flow, versus achieving maximum output in the future (i.e., the relative size of w_1, w_2, and w_3 versus w_4), (2) the relative effects of the interest rate on speculation and gold flows versus its effect on future output (i.e., the relative size of b_{12}, b_{22}, and b_{32} versus b_{42}), and (3) how badly the Fed dislikes to purchase or sell government securities in the open market (i.e., the size of w5). The dilemma of whether the coefficient of ΔGS_t is positive or negative therefore reflects the policy dilemma facing the Fed—which goal or goals to try to achieve when the goals conflict, i.e., which goals are the most important.

In order that the analysis may produce definite signs in the resulting equation for open market operations, it is assumed that, for one or more of the reasons implied in the preceding paragraph, the coefficient of ΔGSt which is divided into both sides of the above equation, is negative. Furthermore, this same problem is apparent in the coefficients of several of the variables in the above equation. It is assumed that the signs attached to the coefficients in the above are the prevailing signs. (After division by the negative coefficient on ΔGS_t the signs will be the opposite of what they are above.)

There is an added problem in obtaining the implied signs of the coefficients of SS_{t-1}, O_t, $\dot{P}_t$ and $S\dot{P}_t$. Since these variables all add to the increased demand for credit, an increase in one or more of them will increase the rate of interest. This increase would partially choke off further increases and thus partially achieve the Fed's assumed countercyclical and anti-speculative goals. But the assumption is made here that the Fed would nevertheless pursue a further increase in the interest rate. This yields negative signs on SS_{t-1}, O_t, $\dot{P}_t$, and $S\dot{P}_t$ in the final equation below. (This is the same problem encountered in the previous section explaining the assumption of the signs in Model I.)

The resulting equation for minimizing the policy makers' disutility is therefore:

$$\Delta GS_t = \pm A_0 - A_1 SS_{t-1} - A_2 S\dot{P}_t - A_3 O_t - A_4 SC_{t-1}$$

$$- A_5 \dot{P}_t - A_6 r_{L_t} + A_7 BT_t + A_8 \Delta G_{t-1} + A_9 G_{t-1} - A_{10} ERS_t$$

$$+ A_{11} DG_t + A_{12} \Delta RR_t' - A_{13}\, \Delta dr_{t-1} + A_{14}\, \Delta ar_{t-1}$$

$$+ A_{15} \Delta dr_t + A_{16} \Delta ar_t + A_{17} B_{t-1} + A_{18} dr_{t-1}$$

$$+ A_{19} ar_{t-1} \qquad \text{(II.10)}$$

Changes in the discount rate. The procedure is once again the same as before. This time, we take the derivative of (II.1) with respect to Δdr_t to obtain

$$\frac{\partial d_t}{\partial \Delta dr_t} = 2w_1 SS_t \frac{\partial SS_t}{\partial \Delta dr} + 2w_2 SC_t \frac{\partial SC_t}{\partial \Delta dr_t}$$

$$+ 2w_3 \Delta G_t \frac{\partial \Delta G_t}{\partial \Delta dr_t} - 2w_3 \Delta G_t * \frac{\partial \Delta G_t}{\partial \Delta dr_t}$$

$$- 2w_4 O_{t+k} \frac{\partial O_{t+k}}{\partial \Delta dr_t} + 2w_6 \Delta dr_t$$

The relevant partials are

$$\frac{\partial SS_t}{\partial \Delta dr_t} = -b_{12}l_6 \qquad \frac{\partial SC_t}{\partial \Delta dr_t} = -b_{22}l_6$$

$$\frac{\partial \Delta G_t}{\partial \delta dr_t} = b_{32}l_6 \qquad \frac{\partial O_{t+k}}{\partial \Delta dr_t} = -b_{43}l_6$$

As could have been predicted, the partials with respect to Δdr_t have the opposite signs than the same partials with respect to ΔGS_t. The reason is, of course, the negative relationship between r_t and ΔGS_t as opposed to the positive relationship between r_t and Δdr_t.

It does not seem necessary to tax the reader any further with another long derivation. The procedure is the same as for open market operations; and making the same assumptions about the signs as were made in that derivation, the result will be the same except that the corresponding variables are expected to have the opposite signs from those in equation (II.10).

Therefore, only the results of the present derivation are presented. The equation for changes in the discount rate is

$$\begin{aligned} \Delta dr_t = &\pm B_0 + B_1 SS_{t-1} + B_2 \dot{S}P_t + B_3 O_t + B_4 SC_{t-1} \\ &+ B_5 \dot{P}_t + B_6 r_{L_t} - B_7 BT_t - B_8 \Delta G_{t-1} - B_9 G_{t-1} \\ &+ B_{10} ERS_t - B_{11} DG_t - B_{12} \Delta N_t + B_{13} \Delta dr_{t-1} \\ &- B_{14} \Delta ar_{t-1} - B_{15} \Delta ar_t - B_{16} B_{t-1} - B_{17} dr_{t-1} \\ &- B_{18} ar_{t-1} \qquad \text{(II.11)} \end{aligned}$$

Changes in the acceptance rate. The derivative of (II.1) with respect to Δar_t is

$$\frac{\partial d_t}{\partial \Delta ar_t} = 2w_1 SS_t \frac{\partial SS_t}{\partial \Delta ar_t} + 2w_2 SC_t \frac{\partial SC_t}{\partial \Delta ar_t}$$

$$+ 2w_3 \Delta G_t \frac{\partial \Delta G_t}{\partial \Delta ar_t} - 2w_3 \Delta G_t * \frac{\partial \Delta G_t}{\partial \Delta ar_t}$$

$$- 2w_4 O_{t+k} \frac{\partial O_{t+k}}{\partial \Delta ar_t} + 2w_7 \Delta ar_t$$

where

$$\frac{\partial SS_t}{\partial \Delta ar_t} = -b_{12}l_7 \qquad \frac{\partial SC_t}{\partial \Delta ar_t} = -b_{22}l_7$$

$$\frac{\partial \Delta G_t}{\partial \Delta ar_t} = b_{32}l_7 \qquad \frac{\partial O_{t+k}}{\partial \Delta ar_t} = -b_{42}l_7$$

Again presenting only the result:

$$\Delta ar_t = \pm C_0 + C_1 SS_{t-1} + C_2 \dot{S}P_t + C_3 O_t$$

$$+ C_4 SC_{t-1} + C_5 \dot{P}_t + C_6 rL_t - C_7 BT_t$$

$$- C_8 \Delta G_{t-1} - C_9 G_{t-1} + C_{10} ERS_t - C_{11} DG_t$$

$$- C_{12} \Delta N_t + C_{13} \Delta dr_{t-1} - C_{14} \Delta ar_{t-1}$$

$$- C_{15} \Delta dr_t - C_{16} B_{t-1} - C_{17} dr_{t-1}$$

$$- C_{18} ar_{t-1} \qquad \text{(II.12)}$$

Bibliography

1. Anderson, Clay J. *A Half-Century of Federal Reserve Policymaking, 1914-1964*. Philadelphia: Federal Reserve Bank of Philadelphia, 1965.

2. Anderson, Leonall C. "Money Market Conditions as a Guide for Monetary Management." *Targets and Indicators of Monetary Policy*. Edited by Karl Brunner. San Francisco: Chandler Publishing Co., 1969.

3. Bonomo, Vittorio, and Charles Schotta. "A Spectral Analysis of Post-Accord Federal Open Market Operations." *American Economic Review*, LIX (March 1969): pp. 50-61.

4. Brunner, Karl, and Allan H. Meltzer. *The Federal Reserve's Attachment to the Free Reserve Concept: A Staff Analysis*. Report of the Subcommittee on Domestic Finance, Committee on Banking and Currency, House of Representatives, 88th Congress, 2nd session. Washington, D.C.: U.S. Government Printing Office, 1964.

5. ——. "What Did We Learn From the Monetary Experience of the United States in the Great Depression?" *Canadian Journal of Economics*, I (May, 1968): pp. 334-348.

6. Burgess, W. Randolph, ed. *Interpretations of Federal Reserve Policy in the Speeches and Writings of Benjamin Strong*. New York: Harper and Brothers, 1930.

7. ——. *The Reserve Banks and the Money Market.* New York: Harper and Brothers Publishers, 1927.

8. Chandler, Lester V. *Benjamin Strong, Central Banker.* Washington, D.C.: The Brookings Institution, 1958.

9. Clarke, Stephen V.O. *Central Bank Cooperation: 1924-1931.* New York: Federal Reserve Bank of New York, 1967.

10. Davenport, Donald H., and Frances V. Scott. *An Index to Business Indices.* Chicago: Business Publications, Inc., 1937.

11. Friedman, Milton, and Anna J. Schwartz. *A Monetary History of the United States, 1867-1960.* Princeton: Princeton University Press, 1963.

12. Goldberger, Arthur S. *Econometric Theory.* New York: John Wiley and Sons, Inc., 1964.

13. Goldenweiser, E.A. "Instruments of Federal Reserve Policy." *Banking Studies.* Edited by U.S. Board of Governors of the Federal Reserve System. Baltimore: Waverly Press, Inc., 1941.

14. Hardy, Charles O. *Credit Policies of the Federal Reserve System.* Washington, D.C.: The Brookings Institution, 1932.

15. Jenkins, Gwilym M., and Donald G. Watts. *Spectral Analysis and Its Applications.* San Francisco: Holden-Day, 1968.

16. Keran, Michael W. and Christopher T. Babb. "An Explanation of Federal Reserve Actions (1933-68)." *Review of the Federal Reserve Bank of St. Louis,* 51 (July, 1969): pp. 7-20.

17. Malinvaud, E. *Statistical Methods of Econometrics. Studies in Mathematical and Managerial Economics,* Vol. VI. Amsterdam: North-Holland Publishing Company, 1966. Chicago: Rand McNally and Company, 1966.

18. Miller, Adolph C. "Responsibility for Federal Reserve Policies: 1927-1929." *American Economic Review*, XXV (September 1935): pp. 442-458.

19. *Statistical Abstract for the United Kingdom (1913 and 1922-35)*. London: H.M. Stationary Office, 1937.

20. Theil, Henri. *Optimal Decision Rules for Government and Industry. Studies in Mathematical and Managerial Economics, Vol. I*. Amsterdam: North-Holland Publishing Company, 1964. Chicago: Rand McNally and Company, 1964.

21. U.S. Board of Governors of the Federal Reserve System. *Banking and Monetary Statistics*. Washington, D.C.: U.S. Board of Governors, 1943.

22. ——. *Open Market Investment Policy: Excerpts, 1923-1928*. Washington, D.C.: U.S. Board of Governors, 1956.

23. ——. *Open Market Investment Policy: Excerpts, 1929 - Mid-1931*. Washington, D.C.: U.S. Board of Governors, 1956.

24. ——. *The Federal Reserve System: Purposes and Functions*. Washington, D.C.: U.S. Board of Governors, 1963.

25. U.S. Bureau of the Census. *Historical Statistics of the United States, 1789-1945*. Washington, D.C.: U.S. Government Printing Office, 1949.

26. U.S. Department of Commerce. *Annual Supplement to the Survey of Current Business, 1932*. Washington, D.C.: U.S. Government Printing Office, 1933.

27. U.S. Federal Reserve Board. *Ninth Annual Report.* Washington, D.C.: U.S. Government Printing Office, 1923.

28. ——. *Tenth Annual Report.* Washington, D.C.: U.S. Government Printing Office, 1924.

29. ——. *Eleventh Annual Report.* Washington, D.C.: U.S. Government Printing Office, 1925.

30. ——. *Twelfth Annual Report.* Washington, D.C.: U.S. Government Printing Office, 1926.

31. ——. *Thirteenth Annual Report.* Washington, D.C.: U.S. Government Printing Office, 1927.

32. ——. *Fourteenth Annual Report.* Washington, D.C.: U.S. Government Printing Office, 1928.

33. ——. *Fifteenth Annual Report.* Washington, D.C.: U.S. Government Printing Office, 1929.

34. ——. *Sixteenth Annual Report.* Washington, D.C.: U.S. Government Printing Office, 1930.

35. ——. *Seventeenth Annual Report.* Washington, D.C.: U.S. Government Printing Office, 1931.

36. ——. *Eighteenth Annual Report.* Washington, D.C.: U.S. Government Printing Office, 1932.

37. ——. *Nineteenth Annual Report.* Washington, D.C.: U.S. Government Printing Office, 1933.

38. ——. *Twentieth Annual Report.* Washington, D.C.: U.S. Government Printing Office, 1934.

39. ——. *Twenty-first Annual Report.* Washington, D.C.: U.S. Government Printing Office, 1935.

40. Wicker, Elmus R. "Federal Reserve Monetary Policy, 1922-1933: A Reinterpretation." *Journal of Political Economy,* LXXIII (August 1965): pp. 324-343.

41. ——. *Federal Reserve Monetary Policy, 1917-1933.* New York: Random House, 1966.

42. Wood, John H. "A Model of Federal Reserve Behavior." *Monetary Process and Policy: A Symposium.* Edited by George Horwich. Homewood: Richard D. Irwin, Inc., 1967.

Index